Chocolate

Sweet Science and Dark Secrets

of the World's Favorite Treat

BY KAY FRYDENBORG

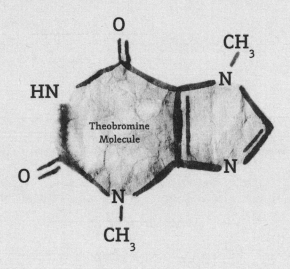

Theobromine
Molecule

HOUGHTON MIFFLIN HARCOURT
BOSTON   NEW YORK

To all people living
in cacao-growing regions,
both in our own time and in the past,
who sacrificed everything in the
name of chocolate.

And to those who have found pleasure
and comfort in a taste of
the world's most perfect food.

Library of Congress Cataloging-in-Publication Data is on file.

ISBN: 978-0-544-17566-2

Manufactured in the United States
DOC 10 9 8 7 6 5 4 3 2 1
4500521553

Contents

The World's
Most Perfect Food

*Chemically speaking, chocolate really is
the world's most perfect food.*

—Michael Levin, nutritional researcher,
as quoted in *The Emperors of Chocolate*, 2000

On April 25, 1947, four boys in the sleepy town of Ladysmith, British Columbia, on Canada's Vancouver Island, decided to take matters into their own hands. They'd discovered that the spare change they'd set aside to buy their favorite chocolate bars from a local ice cream parlor called the Wigwam would no longer be enough to buy the bars. One member of the group, seventeen-year-old Parker Williams, had entered the shop in eager anticipation and had come out empty-handed. Overnight, the price of chocolate bars had risen from five cents to eight cents—a 60 percent increase for a three-ounce bar. Parker could hardly believe his eyes. It was outrageous.

The boys vowed to do something about it that very day. They'd organize a strike! With the friends, classmates, and younger brothers and sisters they had recruited, they scrawled their objections with markers

In 1947, children and teens walked picket lines to protest a sudden hike in the cost of chocolate bars.

on cardboard. They chalked slogans all over Parker's old Buick, too, and later that day he drove this protest-banner-on-wheels slowly up and down the street in front of the Wigwam, while other kids hung off the sides of the car or marched behind. Lifting their signs high, a growing line of youthful militants snaked past shops and passersby, singing lyrics they had just composed:

We want a 5-cent chocolate bar.
8 cents is going too darn far
We want a 5-cent chocolate bar
Oh, we want a 5-cent bar!

World War II had come to an end, and nations around the globe were rebuilding their economies. In the West, free-market capitalism was rushing back after years of government-mandated wage and price freezes — including a freeze on the price of chocolate. Parents were worried about rising prices too.

Most parents in Ladysmith supported their children's protest effort. Many adult-led community groups also began helping out, printing signs and pledge cards, providing snacks for kids on the frontlines, and lending moral support. Chocolate bars, in 1947, seemed like a fundamental right.

Ladysmith was a small town and news traveled fast. Soon nearly every kid in town had joined the "chocolate bar strike." A photographer from the local paper snapped a photo of the protesters circling in front of the Wigwam; the next day, kids across Canada began picketing their own corner stores.

"What this country needs is a good 5-cent bar!" said some of their signs. "Candy is dandy, but 8 cents isn't handy!"

On April 30, two hundred kids marched on British Columbia's capitol building in Victoria and shut down all business in the city for a day because of chocolate. Similar actions were repeated in Burnaby, in Toronto, and on Ottawa's Parliament Hill. The movement swept through the country. Police were called in to break up the crowds. More than three thousand kids signed pledge cards promising to boycott the sale of chocolate until the price returned to normal. Within days, sales of chocolate bars in Canada had dropped by a staggering 80 percent.

Candy companies, caught off-guard, defended the higher price. They, too, were struggling with postwar inflation. The cost of milk, sugar, and cocoa-processing labor had all risen with the lifting of government price controls.

The young protesters were unmoved by this logic. This was about freedom, prosperity, and fairness! It was simple. They wanted their chocolate bars; they *deserved* their chocolate bars. But they would boycott *eight*-cent bars. By raising their collective voices, they aimed to hold the line on runaway prices. They planned their biggest event yet — a march on Toronto — for May 3. But then the adult world of international and domestic politics, big business, and postwar paranoia intervened.

On the eve of the Toronto march, an anonymous source told a reporter at the *Toronto Evening Telegram* that the entire candy strike was being orchestrated by a pro-labor organization with alleged ties to the Communist Party, and the ultraconservative newspaper concluded, in print, that the children's chocolate crusade was nothing more than a front for Communists in Moscow.

Communism was widely feared at that time— many in North America believed that Communists, called "Reds" for their supposed allegiance to the red Soviet flag, were planning to overthrow democracy.

Suddenly, formerly supportive organizations disowned the strike. Emotions were running high, but no one wanted to be seen as a Communist sympathizer. Parents forbade their children to participate further in the demonstrations. The strike fizzled out, and the price of a chocolate bar never returned to five cents. This was deeply disappointing to the kids, for whom communism was an abstract concept that had nothing to do with their spontaneous protest.

But they weren't ready to give up chocolate. Whether allowances were raised by sympathetic parents or extra chores were completed to earn the money, kids continued to buy their favorite bars. By 1947, life

By the time U.K. chocolate maker Divine ended production of Dubble Bars in May 2014, more than 11,000 bars had been sold, contributing more than $162,000 to Fair Trade farmers and development programs, underscoring their slogan, "Changing the World Chunk by Chunk."

without chocolate had become unthinkable—chocolate had already changed the world.

////////////

The truth is, the world has changed chocolate, too, in surprising ways. It's all part of the long, strange history of this remarkable food. In its original liquid, unsweetened form, it was a key element in the culture, diet, religious rituals, and economies of several major Mesoamerican civilizations for more than two thousand years before anyone in the Western world had ever heard of it, let alone tasted a drop.

It wasn't until August 15, 1502, during his fourth and last voyage to the Americas, that Christopher Columbus encountered a large dugout canoe near an island off the coast of what is now Honduras. It was filled with local goods intended for trade, including fine cotton garments, a variety of weapons, and copper bells. But perhaps the most valuable item was a large cache of cacao beans, which Columbus and his men had never seen before and mistook for almonds. Columbus directed his crew to seize the canoe from the Indians and retained their leader as his guide.

Later, Columbus's son Ferdinand described the encounter. He was struck by how much value the Native Americans placed on the strange-looking almonds. "They seemed to hold these almonds at a great price," he wrote, "for when they were brought on board ship together with their goods, I observed that when any of these almonds fell, they all stooped to pick it up, as if an eye had fallen."

What Ferdinand and the other members of Columbus's crew didn't know was that dried cacao seeds were the local currency. They were as precious as cash; in fact, they *were* cash! Though Columbus took some of them back to Spain with the other treasures he acquired (or stole) in the New World, the Spanish court was initially as unimpressed as Columbus himself had been.

It was almost twenty years later that the swashbuckling Spanish conquistador Hernán Cortés arrived on southeastern Mexico's Yucatán Peninsula and quickly began to understand the true value of these unappetizing brown beans the natives prized so highly. It was almost too good to be true: in this new land, money really did grow on trees!

From that time forward, chocolate began sweeping the globe and reshaping the world. Far more than a dessert, it is the basis of a worldwide business that yields annual profits of $83 billion. The average European eats 24 pounds (11 kg) of chocolate per year. In the United States, more than 11 pounds (5 kg) of chocolate are consumed annually by the average U.S. citizen.

But statistics tell only a part of the story. Chocolate has been considered, at various times, to be a sustaining food, strengthening (and sometimes intoxicating) beverage, culinary seasoning, currency, religious icon, status symbol, military ration, guilty pleasure, health food, aphrodisiac, pharmaceutical, and cosmetic. Chocolate has provided inventors and entrepreneurs with great wealth, archaeologists with clues to the lifestyles of people of ancient times, and biologists with insights into the evolution of animals and plants. The new science of chocolate leads back, into a fascinating past with surprising twists and turns, and forward, into the still-evolving future of a warming planet—a planet that is teeming with more than 7 billion people and counting—most of whom want chocolate!

The question is, where in the world did chocolate originate? And how did it go from being a wrinkly brown bean in the hold of an Indian canoe to a universally beloved food in a class of its own, the frustrated desire for which could almost bring business as usual in a major, modern industrial country such as Canada to its knees?

To find out, we have to start in the cocoa woods, where the long-standing human love affair with chocolate began.

THE "NEW" WORLD?

Though he had an abundance of confidence, Christopher Columbus was a confused man on a lofty mission for the queen of Spain. His goal was to reach India, and thus chart a faster and safer trade route for procuring precious silks, spices, and other treasure from the Far East Asian "Indies" (so called because they were near India), but he fundamentally miscalculated his own route. Using outdated and discredited charts and maps, Columbus had estimated the distance around the equator to be sixteen thousand miles, when in reality it is twenty-five thousand miles. Thus he believed that the shimmering island in the Bahamas that he saw on October 12, 1492, was one of the islands in the Far East that Marco Polo had described a century before. The Indies, at last! Having finally spotted land after a difficult ten weeks at sea, Columbus was sure that China and Japan lay just a bit farther north, well within reach.

Returning the following spring with a grand fleet of seventeen ships and a thousand men, he landed on the Caribbean island he named Hispaniola (today's Dominican Republic and Haiti). Though the natives who lined the beach, watching his approach, were the Tainos, a group of some five hundred thousand Arawak Native Americans who had been living there for five thousand years, and though the island was in reality nine thousand miles from India, the disoriented Columbus called the people Indians. The name he bestowed on them stuck, and was later used by Europe-

Christopher Columbus (1451–1506), explorer, navigator, and colonizer, in an engraving by I. W. Baumann, published in *The Book of the World* (Germany, 1851).

ans, and by the European settlers of North America, to describe all the native peoples of this so-called New World.

Many modern scholars believe that more people were living in the Americas at the time than in all of Europe! The central Mexican plateau, realm of the Aztec Empire, may have had a population of 25 million, compared to fewer than 10 million in Spain and Portugal combined. This would have made Mexico the most densely populated place on earth, with more residents per square mile than either China or India. And yet the entire large, native population of a continent, home to diverse civilizations as advanced as any in Europe, was named on the basis of a mistake.

Columbus went to his grave believing, against much evidence to the contrary, that he had, in fact, arrived on the shores of Asia. But even before his death in 1506, his assertion that he had found the Indies was increasingly doubted by others, and he fell out of favor. In the end, the New World was named not for Columbus, but for his acquaintance and fellow Italian explorer Amerigo Vespucci, who recognized that this was, at least for Europeans, a whole new world.

The Cocoa Woods:
Back to Before

*The cocoa woods were another thing.
They were like the woods of fairy tales,
dark and shadowed and cool. The cocoa-
pods, hanging by thick, short stems,
were like wax fruit in brilliant green and
yellow and red and crimson and purple.*

—V. S. Naipaul, *The Middle Passage*, originally published 1962

The tree grows wild—single and scattered, or in ir-
regular clumps all but hidden beneath the tall rainforest canopy of northwestern South America. Able
to survive only within a narrow range of equatorial
conditions, it's fragile, but it's also perfectly adapted
to its rainforest habitat. The tree's leaves can shift
position, from vertical to horizontal and back again,
like a window shutter, providing needed access to
the sun yet protection from sunburn for tender young
leaves. The tree loves damp places, often cluster-
ing near the banks of rivers. Moisture drips from its
broad, flat green leaves and clings to its delicate new

ones, which unfurl in a shiny, deep crimson color that affords further protection from the tropical sun. Moss and lichens cling to the bark of its trunk, as do other plants such as small orchids.

Even before people first saw the tree's multicolored, football-shaped pods festooned like party lanterns up and down the trunk, non-human animal species were drawn to the delicious, tart-sweet pulp. For perhaps fifteen thousand years, scientists believe, forest creatures such as squirrels, monkeys, and bats have feasted on the nutritious and tasty fruit of the tree we call *Theobroma cacao*. They crack or claw or

Cacao is native to the Amazon rainforest ecosystem, which is shared by a multitude of plants and animals.

YOU SAY COCOA, AND I SAY CACAO

Cacao or cocoa? It can be confusing! Chocolate is derived from the cacao (pronounced *kak-kow*) tree, also known by its taxonomic name, *Theobroma cacao*. Cacao seeds (usually called "beans") grow inside the tree's fruit (called "pods"). Once the beans have been dried and fermented, they are referred to as cocoa (pronounced *ko-ko*) and are ready to be processed into cocoa powder, cocoa butter, or chocolate.

So the tree is cacao, and cocoa is the substance that is made from the seeds of the tree. The parts of the cacao tree that are not processed into cocoa, such as the leaves and flowers, remain cacao.

And we shouldn't confuse *either* of these terms with coca (pronounced *ko-ka*), the evergreen shrub from which the drug cocaine is made.

gnaw open the pods, drop or knock them to the ground to break them apart, then dig into the juicy, cream-colored tissue inside. They slurp and nibble the slippery flesh, and spit out the thirty to forty large, bitter seeds arranged neatly within it. Or they swallow the seeds whole. Either way, the tree is happy (if, indeed, a tree can feel happiness), because within days, many of the seeds will take root in leaf-littered, shallow soil, and eventually they will grow new trees.

At the age of three or four, young cacao trees sprout clusters of tiny white flowers that decorate their dark trunks like small, bright stars. Once the cacao tree begins to flower, it will continue to flower year round. The moisture in these flowers evaporates rapidly in the rainforest, and the volatile oils that remain in the flowers have a mushroomy fragrance, so subtle that humans can barely detect it. Tiny biting flies called midges, attracted by the fragrance, enter the flowers, often just before dawn, to sefi nourishment from the sticky, yellowish, high-protein pollen hidden within their stamens. Midges live close to the rainforest floor, on decaying vegetation and organic material beneath a towering canopy of fruit- and flower-bearing trees whose leaves provide dense cover. The flies — each one small enough to fit easily on the head of a pin — whir with the fastest wing beat of any creature

Delicate white and pink flowers resembling miniature orchids sprout directly from the trunk and main branches of the cacao tree.

on earth—up to an astonishing thousand beats a second! But to the tree, all that matters is that midges are the all-important fertilizers, critical to its life cycle. They transfer the reproductive material, pollen, from plant to plant, to maintain diversity.

The pollinated cacao flowers put forth fruit in about forty days, and the fruit pods mature and grow to full size in another five or six months. Even after the pods ripen, changing from mottled green to yellow, crimson, or purple, they remain attached to the trunk of the cacao tree until someone—an animal with claws and teeth, or a human with a machete—cuts them down. Dead leaves and decaying, abandoned pods beneath the trees provide the perfect breeding ground for new midges that will pollinate more cacao flowers; animals, wind, and nearby river currents scatter the tree's seeds throughout the rainforest.

The plant genus *Theobroma* is millions of years old; its birthplace is the Upper Amazon Basin of South America, just east of the great Andes mountains. The cacao tree is one of about twenty-two species of *Theobroma*. Fifteen of these produce edible fruit. But the cacao tree is easily the most important and best-loved *Theobroma* species the world over, because it's the only one whose seeds can make chocolate.

///////////////

No one knows for sure whether the tree that gives us chocolate arose by lucky chance in nature, or whether it emerged from deliberate crossings of related *Theobroma* species by some of the South American continent's first orchard gardeners. Is it merely coincidence that *Theobroma cacao* first appeared in the Amazon Basin (also known as Amazonia) at roughly the same time that humans first arrived in this land some ten thousand to fifteen thousand years ago? If so, it was a most fortunate coincidence, but hardly unique. Despite its poor topsoil — loamy clay depleted and drained by frequent, heavy downpours — the Amazon rainforest gave birth to many of humankind's oldest and most important plant foods, including corn, squash, peppers, mangoes, peanuts, coconuts, figs, sweet potatoes, ginger, nutmeg, vanilla, pineapple, bananas, and many more. The fruits, roots, and seeds of these plants were staples of the local diet long before Spanish explorers encountered them for the first time in the fifteenth century.

The first human inhabitants of this complex rainforest ecosystem (which now comprises the countries of Peru, Colombia, Ecuador, and parts of Bolivia and Venezuela) were likely attracted to bright cacao pods just as animals that lived in the rainforest were. Watching them open the pods and feed on their fruity insides, humans naturally would have tried cracking open the pods for themselves, just as they added other fruits and nuts of the forest to their diet.

Cacao pulp is refreshingly moist and pleasantly acidic, like a lemon. It's thirst-quenching and high in energy-giving sugars. For the people of the Amazon Basin, it was a tantalizing, nutritious snack just wait-

Mesoamerica
and its cultural areas

ing to be cut or pulled from the trees. When they left some of the open cacao pods in the humid air, bacteria and yeast began fermenting sugar into alcohol, and cacao pulp became a beerlike drink called chicha, which is still a popular beverage in parts of South and Central America.

By about 1800 B.C., if not earlier, the native range of cacao trees had expanded westward and northward. From northwestern South America, *T. cacao* had spread to Mesoamerica, the geographical and cultural area that extends from present-day Central Mexico down through Central America, and which includes Guatemala, Belize, Honduras, and El Salvador. Natural forces (seed dispersal by humans, forest animals, and river currents), along with human trade routes, probably account for the tree's spread from its place of origin. Somewhere along the way, an unlikely discovery was made: as delicious as the fruit pulp of the cacao tree was to eat, it was the seeds buried within, long discarded, that were its real, hidden treasure.

No written records exist to tell us how Mesoamericans thousands of years ago hit upon a way to turn seemingly worthless, bitter seeds into what became their most precious drink, and scholars have puzzled over this mystery ever since.

How *did* they do it? How did they learn how to transform trash seeds into a highly valued, even cherished, food?

//////////////////

We can only speculate on the answer. Maybe it happened something like this: At least fifteen hundred years ago, somewhere in the land we now call Central America — perhaps in the southeastern part of the modern-day Mexican state of Veracruz — a member of the Olmec nation, Mexico's first major civilization, picks one of the odd-looking, blimp-shaped fruits that jut out from the smooth-barked trunk of a familiar rainforest tree. Later, around the fire on which dinner is cooked, she opens the pod with a sharp-edged stone tool. Perhaps the pod has been ripening on the tree a bit too long, and the normally fresh, juicy white pulp has become slightly fermented; the almondlike seeds are starting to dry out. The taste is off, so she spits the seeds into the fire, or even tosses the entire opened fruit onto the embers. Maybe it's easier and neater to dispose of rejected pods and seeds in this way than to carry them away with other trash. In any case, the cacao beans begin to roast. Perhaps the Olmec woman begins to notice an unfamiliar aroma.

What is that smell?

She peers into the flames and remembers the now-browning cacao seeds; she carefully rakes them out of the fire before they blacken and shrivel. Again she inhales the wonderful scent and wonders. She sets the roasted beans down to cool on a flat stone in the night air and later, curious, crushes them on a flat, hollowed-out grinding stone, like corn. The rich smell is pleasing. She tastes a bit of the crushed bean paste on her moistened finger. It's bitter, but . . . interesting. She begins to plan how she might use it in food she prepares for her family—perhaps she will mix it with the ground corn!

In such a fortuitous meeting of cacao seed and flame began humankind's long infatuation with chocolate.

Tree of Myth
and Money

From time to time the men of Montezuma's
guard brought him, in cups of pure gold,
a drink made from the cacao-plant,
which they said he took before visiting
his wives. I saw them bring in a good fifty
large jugs of chocolate, all frothed up,
of which he would drink a little.

—Bernal Díaz del Castillo, *The Discovery*
and Conquest of Mexico, 1520

How ancient Mesoamericans invented chocolate —
a complex food that requires many precisely timed
steps to produce — remains a mystery. But it should
come as no surprise that they did it, considering everything else that these earliest Americans were able
to achieve.

For years, scholars thought the inventors of chocolate were the Maya, who reigned over a large area
of Mesoamerica for about 650 years, from A.D. 250 to
900. A much-studied civilization, the Maya left b›ind
many chocolate-related artifacts that have provided

clues to its importance in their lives. But we now know that the Maya were not the first to make chocolate. They inherited the know-how from an even earlier Mesoamerican culture, a people who had learned how to transform cacao seeds into an amazing food hundreds of years before anyone imagined it existed.

It was in the Soconusco region of southeast Mexico (the southernmost part of the current state of Chiapas) — hot, fertile, and wet — where scientists long believed cacao trees were first cultivated for their seeds. Here lived the first pottery-using inhabitants of Mesoamerica, whom archaeologists call the Barra people. They were simple village farmers who nevertheless left behind sophisticated, delicate, neckless jars that have been radiocarbon-dated to between 1800 and 1400 B.C. But it was the Olmec people, who spoke the same language as the Barra and lived north of them, along the Gulf Coast, who spread the knowledge of chocolate making across Mesoamerica, as many as two thousand years before the Maya. How do we know this? Chemistry.

///////////////

T. cacao is the only plant grown in Mesoamerica that contains both theobromine and caffeine. Scrapings of food residue that clung to a fragment of the earliest known Barra pottery, recovered by archaeologists, tested positive for both of these alkyloids. By using two advanced chemical analysis techniques — liquid chromatography and mass spectrometry — chemist W. Jeffrey Hurst of the Hershey Foods Technical Center in Hershey, Pennsylvania, was able to confirm the signature trace of cacao on the interior of even pre-Olmec serving vessels. They called it *kakawa*. The Olmec may not have been the very first to use cacao in their cuisine, but they perfected its cultivation and preparation, and spread that knowledge throughout

One of the colossal Olmec head sculptures uncovered in Mexico. These carvings are thought to date from 1500 B.C.

the Olmec heartland that lay along the southern Gulf Coast.

Who were the Olmec? Their civilization arose at about 1500 B.C. in the coastal forests of what is now the southern Mexican state of Veracruz. Theirs was the first major Mesoamerican civilization — a distinction reserved for the Maya until about 1940, when the American archaeologist Matthew W. Stirling uncovered the stunning remains of an ancient urban site — the almost hidden city of La Venta. It was not far from the village of Tres Zapotes, where an enormous carved stone head had been found, mostly buried but protruding slightly from the ground.

We don't know what the Olmec called themselves. The word *Olmec* was used by the Aztec, or Mexica, people to refer to their southern neighbors and means, literally, "rubber people," or perhaps "people of the land of rubber." Rubber was among the many things the Olmec people invented; they made it from the sap of the latex-producing tropical tree *Castilla elastica*. From this sap, they fashioned rubber balls that were used in an important ritual game played throughout Mesoamerica.

////////////////

AHEAD OF THEIR TIME

Rubber is just one of the Olmecs' many innovations. They are also credited with creating:

Mesoamerica's first urban center. San Lorenzo had an estimated population, at its height, of thirteen thousand. After San Lorenzo was destroyed (for reasons no one today understands), the Olmec built the much larger La Venta forty miles away. La Venta flourished for eight hundred years as the center of Olmec culture, which radiated throughout Mesoamerica.

A system of writing. A twenty-six-pound stone that was carved by the Olmec and that dates to about 900 B.C. contains the oldest known writing in the Western Hemisphere.

Mathematics and calendars. With an advanced understanding of astronomy and mathematics, the Olmec developed several calendars. One of them corresponds closely to our own 365-day calendar; a separate 260-day sacred calendar was perhaps based on a planetary orbit other than Earth's; and a long-count calendar calculated every day from a starting point in the year 3114 B.C. Devising and using all three calendars at once required another imaginative leap that can be attributed to the Olmec: zero. Centuries before the idea appeared in European writings, the Olmec understood the important concept of zero as a placeholder — the only number that is neither negative nor positive, and the boundary between the two. The Olmec had a particular symbol that resembled a shell to stand for it.

Water and drainage systems. The Olmec constructed an elaborate water system, a buried network of conduits made of long, U-shaped rectangular blocks laid end to end and covered with capstones. One aqueduct provided drinking water to different areas of a settlement, and a separate system carried wastewater away from homes.

Art. In addition to the amazingly lifelike and expressive colossal stone heads they left behind, Olmec artists fashioned life-size jade masks whose stern expressions seem to mirror those of the massive heads.

The Olmec developed basic but effective agricultural techniques, based on a slash-and-burn system: overgrown plots of land were burned to clear them for planting, with the resulting ashes providing fertilizer. Based on archaeological discoveries, they were among the first to cultivate cacao trees. Fisherman farmers, they rotated several crops on a seasonal basis, including maize, beans, peppers, and squash. Interspersed within their large gardens and crop fields, perhaps tucked under the shade of taller forest trees and broad-leaved plants such as bananas, were some of the finest-quality cacao trees ever grown in Meso-america. The beans from these trees' descendants, now called *Criollo*, are today a living link to these early agriculturalists. The beans are delicate and highly prized, and sweeter than other types of cacao beans, with complex flavor notes.

Judging from chemical residue found in ancient Olmec pottery, farmers made a paste from ground, roasted cacao seeds, and from the paste they invented a drink made by mixing the paste with water, corn-meal, chili peppers, and other spices. It was a bitter drink—sugar wasn't yet known in this land—but a refreshing and energizing one. Whether the Olmec drank it hot or cold is unknown to us. Perhaps they enjoyed it both ways.

By about 400 B.C., the Olmec population had dwindled, for reasons unclear today. Speculation as to the cause centers on dramatic environmental changes, volcanic activity, and possibly the degradation of rivers due to agricultural practices. Olmec cities were abandoned, often overgrown and eventually reclaimed by the jungle. But complex new societies had already sprung up, many flourishing alongside the Olmec in neighboring and sometimes overlapping regions. In fact, many archaeologists now question the

A dramatic interplay of light and shadow highlights contours of a sculpted head from the Maya civilization.

long-held "Olmec as mother culture" hypothesis; evidence of Maya ceremonial structures that date from the same period as the major Olmec cities of La Venta and San Lorenzo has led some scholars to the conclusion that the Olmec and Maya were sister cultures, with each group influencing the other as they inevitably interacted. The question of whether the Maya were descendants of the Olmec, or rather contemporaries and trading partners, is still not fully settled. But it is clear that the Maya more fully developed such advancements as writing and astronomical calendars that the Olmec had also invented.

The Maya civilization carried out long-distance trade with many other Mesoamerican cultures, some in central and Gulf Coast Mexico, and others as distant as the Caribbean island–dwelling Tainos and possibly even the inhabitants of the Isthmus of Panama, the bridge linking today's Central and South America. Evidence for these broad trade routes includes gold from Panama found by archaeologists in a sacred Maya temple at Chichén Itzá, and Maya goods such as cacao, salt, seashells, jade, and obsidian in trading points as far away as Guatemala and Belize. Probably as a result of seafaring trade, Maya culture soon spread throughout southern Mexico, Belize, Honduras, and El Salvador, dominating the entire region for more than six hundred years with its complex cultural, political, and religious systems.

From the Olmec tradition, the Maya had learned to make their own chocolate drink. The basic process was similar to the Olmec's method, but the Maya version was prepared in a more complex way. Before serving the drink, the Maya poured a spiced cacao-paste and water mixture back and forth from one vessel to another, often from a height of several feet, until a thick foam developed on top.

The resulting beverage became more than just a drink; it assumed a sacred role, central to the Maya creation myth, as well as a ceremonial one. Dark liquid chocolate was ritually (if not yet literally) associated with human blood. It was also a status symbol: only the elite — mostly royalty and priests — were allowed to drink it. In the tombs of Maya noblemen, pottery vessels have been found bearing the Maya hieroglyph for cacao and inscribed with artwork that shows how the drink was prepared. Analysis by modern scientists has revealed traces of liquid chocolate in these pots. Yet, while chocolate was reserved mainly for the Maya elite, who habitually savored a cup at the end of their meals, it seems likely that even the common people probably enjoyed it during important rituals and gatherings.

The Maya, whose achievements in art, architecture, and writing are well documented, also expanded agricultural practices by building cleverly constructed terraces into their poorly drained lowlands. The terrace system trapped silt from nearby rivers to enrich the soil and increase the productivity of their croplands. It is likely that the Maya also cultivated some of the earliest cacao orchards ever known.

Along with maize, cacao resided at the center of Maya culture. Cacao pods were celebrated in art: images were carved into stone, featured prominently in paintings, and used to decorate elaborate drinking vessels. Maya priests wrote about *kakaw* in their sacred texts and official records, leaving us a clear idea of how they prepared and enjoyed their chocolate.

The foam-topped drink for which they became widely known was by far the most popular use for cacao, but chocolate paste was probably added to foods in other ways as well. Cacao residue has been found in Maya vessels, mixed with various spices and other staples of the Maya diet. Ancient Maya cooks even created a forerunner of the chocolate bar. In the Maya version, ground cacao would be mixed with cornmeal and then packed tightly into small, round slabs, which warriors carried for energy and extra strength in battle.

Cacao was present in every part of Maya life, from beginning to end. In Maya baptismal rites, boys and girls between the ages of three and twelve were anointed with a ground mixture of cacao beans and flowers dissolved in pure water obtained from tree hollows. And when members of the elite reached the end of life, cacao beans and chocolate accessories were tucked into their tombs to help nourish them on their journey to the afterlife.

Cacao trees were so vital to life in this civilization that Maya who were living in the Yucatán, a region normally too dry for cacao trees to grow, figured out a way to grow a few of them anyway. They planted seeds in wet, soil-filled sinkholes that mimicked rainforest habitat by providing their own microclimate of humidity. These mini-plantations were mostly "hobby groves" for the wealthy elite, but cacao beans that were grown in warmer, damper regions were widely traded and were generally available to those who could afford the price.

THE HERO TWINS

We know all this about the early days of chocolate in Maya society because the Maya were not only meticulous artists but also prolific reporters, with a fully developed written language. This language's code has been largely cracked by recent scholarship, but unfortunately, most of the Maya's writings have been lost to history. Of the thousands of books that existed at the time of first contact with the Spanish in the early

In an ancient Maya ball court, the surviving "hoop" is made of solid stone.

sixteenth century, only four survive. Some fell victim to the humid climate, but many were burned by Spanish priests in an attempt to suppress the native religion of the Maya, whom they intended to convert to Christianity. Friar Diego de Landa ordered a bonfire of "idols" and hieroglyphic scrolls and codices that took place on July 12, 1652. Afterward, the friar wrote that as the folding scrolls, which he assumed must be filled with witchcraft and evil knowledge, went up in flames, he noticed in passing that the Maya "regretted to an amazing degree" the destruction of their cultural and sacred record, which "caused them much affliction."

One Maya document that survived is the *Popol Vuh*, or Book of Counsel. It was the sacred book of the Quiché Maya, who lived in the Guatemalan highlands, and it recounts an epic narrative that was probably handed down by word of mouth. Not long after the Spanish conquered these lands, stories of the conquest were recorded by survivors, and it was this version that survived. Some of the stories were transcribed by the Dominican priest Francisco Ximenez in the early 1700s. Ximenez was a linguist who lived for a time in Guatemala, and who was interested in the native language of the Quiché Maya.

The *Popol Vuh* contains many stories of origins and traditions, but one of the most important is the tale of the Hero Twins, the creation myth of the Maya. The story concerns two sets of twins. The first set, sons of the old couple who created the universe in a time before time, meet their untimely end in Xibalba, the underworld of the Maya, where they are beheaded (after losing a ball game) by the Lords of Death. The severed head of one twin, forever after known as the maize god, is hung on a tree that is pictured, on at least one ancient vase, as a cacao tree.

One day this disembodied head magically impregnates the daughter of an underworld king when she touches it with her hand. The girl is expelled in disgrace from the earth, but later gives birth to the second divine set of twins, known as Hunahpu and Xbalanque. These twins are tested again and again by the underworld gods. Finally, in a last-ditch effort to defeat them, the Lords of Death invite them to play a game that involves jumping over a huge fire pit. But the twins willingly jump into the fire together and are burned, and their bones are ground into powder and poured into the river, much as cacao is refined into chocolate. Within five days, the twins are reborn as two fish and emerge from the water as masked magicians who can bring anything back to life, including themselves. They kill the Lords of Death, then rise to the sky in glory as the sun and the moon.

The tale is reflected in a curious way in the Maya word *kakaw*, spelled with two fish symbols, both representing the syllable *ka*. This makes sense to linguists, because the Maya word for "fish" is *kay*, or *kar*. Scribes often used a two-dot duplication symbol before the fish glyph, indicating that the sound was to be repeated twice. But the Maya word for "two" is also *ka*. So two *ka* glyphs together, with the two-dot symbol and the final syllable *wa*, spell *kakaw*.

Is it possible that the ancient Maya myth of the Hero Twins derives from a pun on the word *kakaw*? If so, a three-hundred-year-old witticism may explain the curious use of a fish symbol to stand for cacao in ancient Maya texts and pottery.

The Maya symbol for cacao.

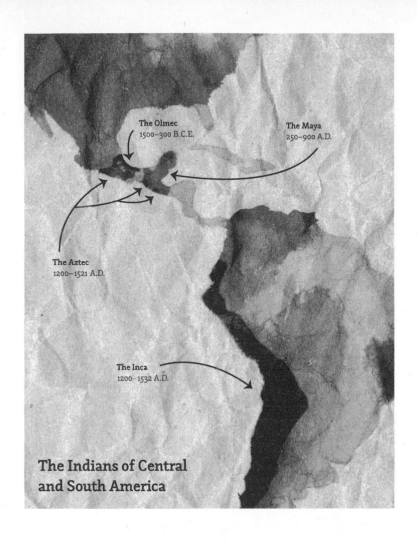

The Olmec
1500–300 B.C.E.

The Maya
250–900 A.D.

The Aztec
1200–1521 A.D.

The Inca
1200–1532 A.D.

The Indians of Central and South America

////////////

The Maya flourished until the end of the ninth century A.D., and then the civilization began to fade and implode—a collapse attributed mainly to overpopulation and extreme environmental degradation. As great Maya cities were abandoned and left to crumble after about A.D. 900, competing cultures, under the sway of chocolate, battled over control of the richest cacao-producing lands and of the trade routes that provided access to these lands.

The people of the last Mesoamerican empire, which came to dominate the region in and around the Valley of Mexico for more than three hundred years, from 1200 to 1521, were even more devoted to the seed of the cacao tree than any of their predecessors. They called themselves the Mexica, but today the world knows them by another name: the Aztecs. This name was based on the Aztecs' own creation legend, which was built on claims to a mythical ancestral homeland somewhere to the north called Aztlán ("Land of the White Herons").

As with the Maya, only Aztec elite could afford to regularly drink chocolate, although unlike the Maya, the Aztecs refused the bitter drink to their priests, who were expected to abstain from earthly pleasures. It was available only to Aztec rulers, nobles, and soldiers, and it was commonly served after feasts in specially decorated cups called *xicalli*, made from calabash gourds. Legend has it that Emperor Motecuhzoma (also spelled Montezuma or Moctezuma) drank fifty golden goblets of hot chocolate, dyed red with ground achiote seeds and flavored with chili peppers, every day. But for the common people, drinking even a cupful was out of the question, because cacao beans were used as currency. Most people couldn't afford to drink their money, which they saved and used to pay the tribute that was demanded by the emperor or traded for their daily needs. For them, cocao beans simply provided purchasing power — a means of survival. They were traded at the city's central market and always kept carefully secured. A rabbit could be bought for between four and ten beans, depending on its freshness and quality; a mule was worth fifty beans; and a turkey hen could cost as much as one hundred beans. Slaves and women also had their price.

Though Columbus had failed to grasp the monetary value of the beans among the Mesoamerican people, his countryman Hernán Cortés, arriving more than a decade after Columbus departed, would not.

///////////////

It was the conquistadors — soldiers, explorers, and adventurers led by the ambitious young Cortés to the shores of Mexico's Yucatán Peninsula in 1519 — who invented the word *chocolate*, or, originally, *chocolatl*.

Only nonnative speakers could have come up with it, by combining the Maya word *chocol*, meaning "hot," and the Nahuatl (Aztec) *atl*, meaning "water." What the Aztecs themselves called it, no one knows for sure. But we do know that chocolate would not exist if not for the inventiveness of ancient Mesoamerican people, some of whose languages we still do not fully understand. Among a handful of New World plants, such as maize, tomatoes, and potatoes, cacao became an early bridge between European culture and the ancient, indigenous peoples of Mesoamerica.

Once that bridge was built, both cultures were forever transformed.

Blood and Chocolate

*This drink is the healthiest thing, and
the greatest sustenance of anything you
could drink in the world, because he who
drinks a cup of this liquid, no matter
how far he walks, can go a whole day
without eating anything else.*

—*A gentleman of Hernán Cortés, 1556*

It must have been a strange sight, the long line of several hundred pale-skinned, bearded men, their leaders astride huge, four-legged animals that the people of the city had never before seen. The riders looked like man-beasts, but they wore fancy dress and metal armor, sat tall in curved saddles of leather and silver, and spoke a language that the Aztecs did not understand.

The date was November 8, 1519, and the place was Tenochtitlán, a magnificent city of more than two hundred thousand inhabitants—one of the largest urban centers in the world at the time. It rose from the sparkling Lake Texcoco, fifty miles long, in the heart of

Mexico. While residents gazed in awe upon their advancing visitors, the men on horseback gaped equally in wonder at what lay before them.

The views in every direction were spectacular. Purple mountains rimmed the clear lake waters, sparkling in the sun and dotted with floating gardens. Against that stunning natural backdrop stretched three straight, raised causeways—spotlessly clean—that led to and from the mainland. On the other side of the causeways lay an urban center unlike anything the Spaniards could have seen in Europe. Two aqueducts supplied fresh water to the city, which also boasted splendid temples and palaces, gardens, aviaries, and zoos. There was a ball court, as well as priests' quarters and schools for training young noblemen for the priesthood. There were administrative offices, markets, and craftsmen of all sorts, and in other neighborhoods outside the city center, there lived the commoners: farmers, laborers, and soldiers.

After descending into the Valley of Mexico from a high mountain pass between volcanoes, the strangers crossed into the city on the southernmost bridge. Hernán Cortés, a brash thirty-four-year-old adventurer and would-be conqueror, was in the lead. They were met at the city gate by none other than the ruler himself, Motecuhzoma II, followed by his retinue of lords and nobles, arrayed in great finery. The Aztecs came on foot, as they always did, since no horses—no domesticated animals of any kind except dogs—existed in their land. Some accounts later claimed that the emperor was carried by his subjects on a special ceremonial litter (a sort of portable throne that rests on poles and that is balanced on the shoulders of soldiers), while others said that he, too, came on foot, flanked by a nobleman on either side, and that he alone among his barefoot people wore golden sandals on his feet.

The emperor, or *tlatoani,* as he was called by his people, was the ninth ruler of Tenochtitlán, then in the seventeenth year of his reign. According to Bernal Díaz del Castillo, who marched with Cortés that day, Motecuhzoma was "of good height, well proportioned, spare and slight, and not very dark, though of the usual Indian complexion. He did not wear his hair long but just over his ears, and he had a short black beard, well shaped and thin. His face was rather long and cheerful, he had fine eyes, and in his appearance and manner could express geniality or, when necessary, a serious composure."

Perhaps because Díaz del Castillo recorded this description nearly fifty years after the day the two groups met, his accounts, and those of Cortés and other Spaniards who were present, contain numerous inconsistencies; it's impossible to know with certainty what took place on the causeway into Tenochtitlán. But it's easy to imagine the scene, given what we do know.

As tall and imposing as the conquistadors on their horses must have seemed to the Aztecs, so the Aztecs, especially Motecuhzoma in his ceremonial headdress, would have appeared to the visitors. The headdress was made of solid gold, ornately engraved, encrusted with jewels, and topped by a spray of deep green plumes. The added height of the feathers would have made the king of the Aztecs appear very tall indeed. And the gold, so lavishly displayed, was proof that the treasure Cortés sought must be here in abundance, just waiting to be taken for the Crown of Spain, and for Cortés himself.

According to accounts later recorded by several of the conquistadors, the first encounter began with the use of ceremonial water for washing hands and the exchange of gifts: tobacco tubes as a sign of friendship, flowers to uplift the spirit, and goblets of chocolate to set the tone and begin a conversation, even though neither man at the center could understand the other. It is said that Cortés gave the Aztec ruler a string of colored glass beads, while Motecuhzoma presented Cortés with an Aztec calendar, a disk of handcrafted gold, and another of silver. According to Díaz del Castillo, Cortés would later melt down these precious metals and add the result to his stolen treasure.

///////////////

In little more than three hundred years, the Aztecs had grown from a small, wandering tribe of nomads, living much as Stone Age peoples had, into the most powerful, aggressive, and dominant force in the Mexican heartland. They had killed and captured many of their enemies in battle; most of those prisoners would eventually become blood sacrifices to the Aztec gods, as would some of the Aztec people themselves. Conquered tribes were forced to pay tribute to the Aztecs in the form of jewels, fine clothing, feathers, and, above all, cocoa beans.

The cacao tree refused to grow in the climate of the Aztec Empire. Though Tenochtitlán carried on a brisk trade with Maya cacao suppliers to the south, it was much easier for the emperor to get what had become a necessity of life by demanding it in tribute. The rulers and nobility of Tenochtitlán had grown wealthy, having shed streams of blood in the process.

When Cortés and 550 Spanish soldiers landed, on April 21, 1519, with a fleet of eleven Spanish galleons on an island off the eastern Gulf Coast near present-day Veracruz, Mexico, they were originally on a mission personally authorized by the Spanish governor of Cuba to explore and secure the interior of Mexico for purposes of colonization. Cortés, though, had fallen out of favor with his former mentor and had taken the expedition into his own hands, defying the governor's attempts to stop him.

After disembarking and setting up camp on the dunes, the Spaniards were met by an initially friendly reception from the local Maya, who gave them gifts of jewels and intricately stitched feathers, and offered a festive meal of grilled fowl, meat, fruit, and special gourds filled with a strange, bitter drink that was not particularly pleasing to the Europeans' palate, but was apparently of great significance to their hosts. It was Cortés's first encounter with chocolate.

//////////////

By the time Cortés and his forces — now including translators, more horses purchased in Trinidad, and

Portrait of the Spanish explorer and conquistador Hernán Cortés (1485–1547), by William Holl (1850).

additional men—arrived at the Aztec capital, they had already defeated several other native groups. They had massacred thousands and made allies of even more, who agreed to join the Spaniards in marching against their hated enemy the Aztecs.

Motecuhzoma's soldiers could easily have overcome the Spanish on that first day. Despite the strangers' horses, allies, and weapons, the Aztecs outnumbered them many times over, and they were fierce, well-armed fighters. But Motecuhzoma chose to be cautious and cordial. He invited the men into his city, sparing no effort to make them comfortable, and even provided them with luxurious lodging in the ancient palace of his father. He overlooked the rudeness of the Spaniards, who ignored at least some of the unspoken rules of the Aztec Empire from either ignorance, arrogance, or both: the ruler was akin to a god; his feet were never to touch the earth; he himself was not to be touched except by his wives and concubines and the nobles of his choice; and no one was ever to look him in the eye.

Some accounts have suggested that the Aztecs may have initially taken Cortés for the god Quetzalcoatl, whose foretold return happened to coincide with the year in which the conquistadors landed on the shores of Mexico. Modern scholars doubt that this is true, but Motecuhzoma must have had his own tactical reasons for the extraordinary restraint he showed toward the invaders.

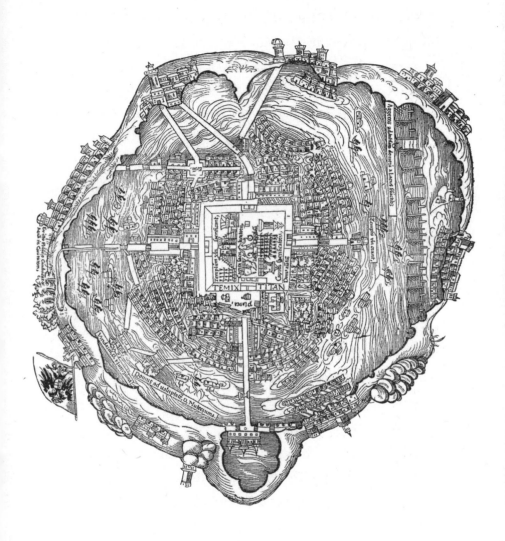

This drawing of Tenochtitlán, the Aztec capital, was published in 1556 and was based on a drawing believed to have been sketched by Hernán Cortés.

Perhaps the emperor even calculated that his lavish gifts would intimidate the conquistadors, or that in getting to know them better, he might understand their weaknesses and crush them more easily later.

But the welcome seemed only to embolden Cortés. It wasn't just his appetite for precious metals and jewels that had been excited. By now, Cortés understood not only that the cacao bean was a thing of great value in this new world, but that with it came power. He observed Motecuhzoma himself daily consuming fifty goblets of chocolate — though probably contained not in the golden goblets of legend but rather in special painted calabash gourds called *xicalli*. In his vast storeroom stood bins containing nearly a billion beans. All of his soldiers were well supplied with chocolate, for strength and stamina, and their victories in battle suggest that it must have been a successful strategy.

On the surface, things went along amicably enough for a while after the Spaniards settled in as pampered guests of the Aztec ruler, but eventually Cortés made a startlingly bold move: he and his men took Motecuhzoma hostage in his own palace and began forcing him to rule his kingdom according to their wishes. The Aztec people responded with increasing anger and resentment.

By the time that day—August 13, 1521—was over, Motecuhzoma was dead, killed either by his own desperate people or by the Spaniards, who realized he was no longer of any use to them. What remained of his dazzling city, his riches, and his vast treasury of cocoa beans fell to Cortés and the Spaniards.

Most of Motecuhzoma's subjects were dead or dying. Some perished in battle or as a result of starvation or disease during the long siege of their city, but most, including Motecuhzoma's unlucky, short-lived successor, his brother Cuitláhuac, died of smallpox, the ghastly disease the Spaniards had inadvertently brought with them. Against that killer, they had no defense. They had never before been exposed to smallpox and to other diseases that were brought to them from the other side of the world, either in the person of the invaders or in the bodies of their unfamiliar animals, and so had no immunity.

The violent fall of Tenochtitlán was the beginning of the end of a way of life for the native peoples of the Americas, occurring, according to the Mesoamerican Long Count Calendar, exactly 4,635 years from the day of creation.

///////////////

Stone calendar, an artifact of the Aztec civilization, found in Mexico.

CHOCOLATE AND THE GODS

Religion lay at the heart of Aztec society, and chocolate played a central role in religious rituals at the time of the Spanish conquest. The Aztecs were polytheists — they worshiped dozens of gods and goddesses, many of whom represented natural and agricultural forces. They also believed in a sort of layered reality of the world throughout time; they, the Aztec people, were living in the time of the fifth (and last) sun, the previous four suns having died. The sun god was the supreme war god, and for good reason. Keeping the fifth sun alive was a huge challenge. Every day, as it rose into the sky, it faced an epic battle with the moon and the stars; its life-giving light was a daily victory, but the battle had to be waged all over again the next morning. It was essential that the people strengthen the sun for this battle by feeding it the energy of life: fresh blood in the form of human sacrifice. It was the only way that the world could be saved anew each day.

Sacrificial victims could come from the ranks of slaves or criminals, but most were prisoners of war. The Aztecs' aggressive wars against their Mesoamerican neighbors were fought not only to expand territory but also to keep a steady supply of candidates for sacrifice. Though the Aztecs were not the first Mesoamerican culture to practice human sacrifice, they carried it out on a much larger scale than the Maya and other civilizations in the region. Perhaps as many as three thousand to four thousand people a year were sacrificed in public ceremonies.

The Aztecs referred symbolically to cacao as *yollotl, extli*, meaning "heart, blood." The cacao pod symbolized the beating human heart, torn from the victim's chest at the moment of sacrifice. The association between the human heart and cacao pods may have relied partly on a slight similarity in shape, but more important, both were vessels that held precious liquids — blood and chocolate.

When Cortés and his conquistadors saw the dried paths of blood that stained the steps of the temple used for sacrifices in the heart of Tenochtitlán, and witnessed some of the sacrifices, they were horrified. But sixteenth-century Spain, as well as England and France in that era, executed a much larger percentage of their populations than did the Aztecs, often before huge crowds that roared their approval. A double standard in regard to violence seemed to guide the Spanish throughout their conquest of Mesoamerica, triumphantly renamed New Spain, and the Aztec sacrifices may have added to the conquerors' sense that they were morally justified in their treatment of the proud people whose lands and lives they had claimed.

Cortés and the conquistadors became the first political powers and large landholders in New Spain. Cortés had learned well the value of money that grows on trees, and he quickly established his own cacao plantation in the name of Spain, the first of many that would be crucial in the coming years as the obsession with chocolate spread from Mesoamerica to Spain, where it would be kept a virtual state secret for a hundred years.

As the conquistadors assumed power, they and the Spanish colonists who followed them began living among the natives, as well as enslaving them. In many cases they married and had children with native women. Thus the first generation of *mestizos* — mixed-blood citizens — was born. With the introduction of cane sugar, grown on a vast scale on the private estates of Cortés, the sweet-toothed Spanish began to truly enjoy their chocolate beverage. At the same time, the surviving Aztecs adjusted to the presence of domestic animals such as cattle, pigs, goats, chickens, and sheep in their midst, as well as fruit trees, including peaches and oranges, that they had never known before. The blending of cultures and tastes had begun.

By the end of the seventeenth century, only 10 percent of the original population of Mesoamerica was still alive. But heirs to chocolate culture — the Maya of Soconusco on the Pacific lowland plain to the south — did live on. As ancient guardians of the world's premier cacao, some Maya even came close to prospering. Unfortunately, the epidemics that were brought on by the arrival of the Spanish had taken their toll on the Maya, too, and as a result, cocoa production dropped sharply just as demand surged. Something had to be done, because for settlers and Mesoamericans alike, chocolate had become a daily necessity.

RECIPE

Aztec Chocolate

Reported by the Anonymous Conqueror,
a.k.a. a gentleman of Hernán Cortés, 1556.

"These seeds which are called almonds or cacao are ground and made into powder, and other small seeds are ground, and this powder is put into a certain basin with a point, and then they put water on it and mix it with a spoon. And after having mixed it very well, they change it from one basin to another, so that a foam is raised which they put in a vessel made for the purpose. And when they wish to drink it, they mix it with certain small spoons or gold or silver or wood, and drink it, and drinking it one must open one's mouth, because being foam one must give it room to subside, and go down bit by bit."

Taming
Wild Amazon Chocolate

*The cacao from Peru is the coin that is
more used; the silver coin is of less use.
With that cacao they buy food in the towns
of the Indians as well as in the towns of
the Spanish. They use it in the Plazas,
butcher shops, and also they buy
chocolate with it. It serves as coin and as
sustenance and because of this it is very
necessary. Without it people cannot live
and if they were to lack cacao, particularly
the poor people, they will perish.*

—Alonzo Diaz, 1626

In 1493, not long after Columbus's failed first voyage
in search of a new trade route to Asia, Pope Alexander VI divided the New World into two parts. In the
following year, an official document called the Treaty
of Tordesillas was signed by Spain and Portugal to
clarify ownership claims to territory in the New World.
According to these two declarations, everything in

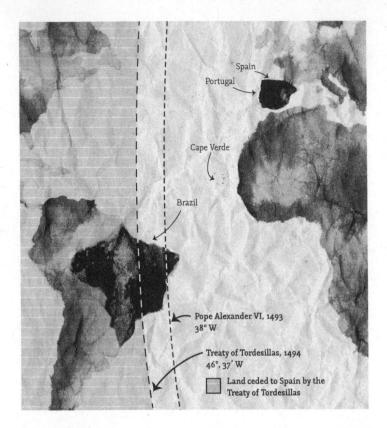

Spain

Portugal

Cape Verde

Brazil

Pope Alexander VI, 1493
38° W

Treaty of Tordesillas, 1494
46°, 37' W

Land ceded to Spain by the
Treaty of Tordesillas

the New World west of an imaginary north–south line went to Spain, and everything east of it was granted to Portugal. Portugal's share of the prize was land that would become Brazil, and Spain got the rest. The original inhabitants of these lands were denied any claim at all.

The new boundaries were really just lines on paper at the time, since hardly anyone in Spain or Portugal had seen the mighty Amazon River or the vast, lush interior of the South American continent now owned in their names. They had no way of knowing until later that Spain had been given a much larger portion of land, but by then the best the Portuguese could do was to push for expanding Brazil's western border as the region became more fully mapped.

The Europeans may not have known what their wild, uncharted territories contained, but high on their lists of valuables to be sent back to their home countries was cacao.

///////////////

By the early seventeenth century, demand for chocolate had risen dramatically in New Spain, as Spanish colonists developed a taste for the native drink, embellished with their own sweeteners and flavorings. In Mexico, chocolate drinking had spread from the wealthy elite to all classes of people, even the clergy. In 1544, a group of Dominican friars who had traveled to the New World to convert the natives to Christianity brought a delegation of Maya nobles from Guatemala across the ocean to visit Prince Philip of Spain. Among the many gifts that the delegation presented to the prince were containers of cocoa beans, and more: the Maya brought gift jars of beaten chocolate, premixed and ready to drink, complete with foam.

Foamed chocolate was not an immediate sensation at the Spanish court. But by 1585 the first commercial shipment of cocoa beans arrived in Seville, carried by Spanish soldiers returning from Veracruz. Soon the Spanish nobility became huge fans of the drink — so much so that they kept chocolate a closely guarded secret within the borders of Spain, restricting its production to monks who were hidden away in monasteries, for nearly a hundred years. The secret was so well kept that when English pirates boarded what they thought was a Spanish treasure ship in 1579, they mistook its huge cache of cocoa beans for a worthless load of dried sheep's droppings. In their frustration, the pirates torched the ship, unwittingly destroying a cargo the likes of which would eventually be worth a small fortune in their own country.

In 1606, a Florentine traveler named Antonio Carletti discovered chocolate while in New Spain. He wrote home that this chocolate drink was taken by both natives and Spaniards, "and any other nationality that goes there." And he explained why:

> Once they start it they become so addicted that it is difficult for them not to drink it every morning, or late in the day when it is hot,

or when on shipboard, because they carry it in boxes, mixed with spices, or made into tablets which dissolve quickly when put in water.

Carletti took some chocolate home to Italy, and the drink proceeded to take Europe by storm. From Italy, the craze spread to Germany, Austria, Switzerland, and France. The Spanish princess Anne of Austria, daughter of King Philip of Spain, presented her husband-to-be, Louis XIII of France, with samples of chocolate in 1615. She also shared samples with other powerful men in the court. The beans, by then, had been spilled. By 1657, the first chocolate house was opened in London by a Frenchman. It was called the Coffee Mill and Tobacco Roll, probably because coffe›ouses were already popular. Chocolate was expensive—ten to fifteen shillings per pound—so it was still reserved for England's wealthy elite.

///////////////

Demand for chocolate was exploding all over Europe just as free or cheap labor in Mesoamerica was plummeting, primarily because of the devastating diseases that had been introduced into the native population. Due to environmental degradation caused largely by plantation-style cacao production, as well as this severe labor shortage, yields of the prized cocoa beans from Guatemala and the ancient Maya groves of Soconusco had fallen to half of what they had been in the previous century. The price of cocoa in Mexico shot up accordingly, and other entrepreneurs rushed in to supply the demand. They began in Ecuador, where Spanish settlers had started arriving not long after Spain's conquest of neighboring Peru in about 1533. Both countries had been part of the vast Inca Empire, about which the conquistadors knew little when they arrived.

At the time, the Peruvian capital, Qosqo (Cuzco), was a large city even more opulent than the one that had dazzled Cortés and his men when they crossed the bridge into Tenochtitlán and entered the kingdom of the Aztecs. At its heart was a huge open plaza carpeted with white sand, carried by workers from the Pacific and raked daily by other workers to pristine perfection. Rising around the plaza were immense stone temples and palaces covered with sheets of polished gold. The sun reflected blindingly off golden walls and shimmering sand. Instead of bridges leading into and out of the city, Qosqo boasted four highways, like geometric spokes extending out from the plaza, marking the four sections of the Inca Empire.

This empire was called Tawantinsuyu, or "Land of the Four Quarters."

Over several hundred years, through a series of stunning conquests of other indigenous peoples that rivaled the speedy rise of the Aztecs in Mexico, the Incas had dramatically enlarged their kingdom, while also developing an advanced, prosperous, and innovative civilization. One example of the latter was their agricultural techniques. They'd invented a sophisticated system of vertical farming—stone-walled terraces carved into mountain slopes—to take advantage of the steep Andean highlands where they lived.

Andean highlands of Peru, where scientists believe cacao originated.

Theirs was a world of valleys, peaks, and high plains, brilliant in contrasts and colors.

Their diet and their crops were equally diverse. Coastal fishing was a primary source of food, but shepherds also herded llamas and alpacas for their meat and wool. The Incas grew a wealth of crops, from cotton and corn to squash, beans, quinoa, potatoes, and tomatoes. Cacao had always grown wild in the rainforests of the Amazon Basin, but its cultivation there was little known, and chocolate, if consumed at all, was far from achieving the status of cultural icon that it had held for centuries in Mesoamerica. That was about to change, along with everything else in the Inca Empire.

The conquistador Francisco Pizarro, a second cousin of Hernán Cortés who shared Cortés's birthplace of Medellín, Spain, had followed his cousin to the New World on news of his great victories, which had unleashed a wave of conquest fever back in Spain. Soon after he reached South America, Pizarro quickly took Puná, near present-day Guayaquil, Ecuador, on the coast. Then he led an advancing force of 168 men, fortified with a full arsenal of guns and swords, plus a cannon and 27 horses. They were met by the Inca king Atawallpa, himself fresh from victory in battle over

An antique illustration of the Spanish explorer and conquistador Francisco Pizarro (ca. 1475–1541).

his own brother, and as many as 6,000 of his soldiers in the central square of the town of Cajamarca.

The Incas carried only ceremonial weapons. Pizarro's guns and horses were hidden inside buildings surrounding the square. When a Spanish priest handed the Inca leader a battered Christian prayer

The Inca emperor Atawallpa in defeat, vanquished by Spanish troops under the leadership of Francisco Pizarro. Engraving from *American History* (1602) by Theodore de Bry (1528–1598).

book, Atawallpa tossed it aside, unable to read it or to understand the significance it held for the strangers. This unwitting gesture unleashed the attack that Pizarro had planned all along. Taken entirely by surprise, the Incas were overwhelmed and confused by the noise and the chaos of gunfire, shouting, and charging horses. Many were trampled to death, and most of the rest died of gunshot wounds. Atawallpa was taken captive by Pizarro himself.

Incredibly, it had happened again. A strong Indian leader had been defeated in battle by an enemy his own forces outnumbered fifty to one, leading to a transformation of power and property the likes of which the Inca could never have imagined.

After the ambush, Pizarro held Atawallpa prisoner in Cajamarca for months, offering to free him if, in exchange, he would order his subjects to fill a large room with gold and two rooms with silver. But in August of 1533, after Atawallpa delivered on his promise to do so, Pizarro ordered his men to strangle the captive king. Then the Spaniards marched to Qosqo, the capital, and seized what remained of it. This time, though, the conquest of an Indian empire would be drawn out and more difficult, with forty years of fierce resistance in outlying regions.

By 1572, the dread disease smallpox had claimed at least half of the native population and had weakened the rest. Epidemics continued to spread from Mesoamerica, where smallpox and other deadly diseases had been introduced by Spaniards to a population with no natural immunity. Once these diseases took hold, they raced through the native communities. In South America, the smallpox infection first introduced into Mesoamerica was so virulent that it had actually arrived in advance of the Spaniards. This and other diseases would all but wipe out vestiges of the Inca civilization in less than fifty years.

//////////////

Ecuador provided the first South American source of cacao for colonists who were eager to exploit its value. It lay just to the north of Peru — that much closer to the already established Spanish settlements in Mesoamerica, with their new, large cacao plantations. The Ecuadorian coastal climate was well suited to the needs of delicate cacao trees; colonists found extensive stands growing wild in the forests along the Guayaquil Gulf Coast.

Early settlers had grown accustomed to the fine *Criollo* (meaning "native") cacao of Mexico; the Ecuadorian cacao was different, and it was called *Forastero* ("foreign"), even though it was native to Ecuador, Peru, and the Amazon Basin. Forastero cacao was abundant and therefore cheap, but often described as inferior. The trees were hardy and produced more fruit than the Criollo variety, but the beans inside their pods were large, dry, and bitter-tasting in comparison. Nevertheless, by the early seventeenth century the

Spaniards had cleared the forest from around these wild Forastero trees and were cultivating them on a large scale.

Meanwhile, the Spanish Crown had begun to impose its rule on the vast new territory it now claimed. Former conquistadors reinvented themselves as land barons and masters of the native population; soon more Spanish colonists began arriving. In New Spain, the Spanish administrative, military, religious, and trade bureaucracies exerted an absolute monopoly on trade. Gold, silver, and agricultural products from the Americas were sent to Spain, and all manufactured goods used in the colonies were to be imported *from* Spain. As for the Indians, they would provide free labor to the colonists through the *encomienda* system, which was administered by local Spanish land barons.

The Spanish word *encomienda* means "to entrust," but the Spanish colonists gave the people whose land and lives they appropriated little basis for trust. Large land grants were given to former conquistadors, settlers, priests, and colonial officials, and with the land came ownership of any native cities, towns, and communities that were established on it, and of any other families who lived there. The natives were expected to provide tribute to those who possessed the land grants, in the form of gold and silver, crops and other foodstuffs, animals such as pigs and llamas, and whatever else the land produced. Natives were also expected to work on the land for a prescribed but often indefinite period of time, on one of the vast sugar cane plantations that the sweets-loving Spaniards had established; in the greatly expanded silver and gold mines; or in agricultural activities such as raising livestock. In return, the land baron, or *encomendero*, was supposedly responsible for the well-being of his subjects, though in practice and intent this generally meant only that the natives were instructed in Christianity in an effort to convert them. All other aspects of their welfare were neglected, at best; abuse and brutality were commonplace.

In Peru, where encomiendas were granted on the ruins of the once rich and mighty Inca Empire, exploitation was particularly severe. The encomenderos showed extreme indifference to the suffering of families on their land. They insisted on produce quotas even when crops failed or natural disasters struck; many natives were forced to choose between fulfilling quotas and starving to death or facing lethal punishment. During the first years of the colonial era, Peruvian natives died by the hundreds of thousands, many specifically from these abuses.

Eventually, under pressure from reformers such as Bartolomé de Las Casas, the Dominican friar who warned of the complete depopulation of Native Americans in New Spain and the eternal damnation of the perpetrators, King Charles V of Spain passed new laws designed to halt the cruelties of the encomienda system. Henceforth, natives were to have certain rights as citizens of Spain and could not be forced to work against their will. "Reasonable" tribute could be collected, but if additional work was required, it was to be compensated. Existing encomiendas would pass back to the Crown upon the death of the encomendero, and no new encomiendas were to be granted. Anyone who could be proven to have abused natives could lose his encomienda. The encomenderos rebelled against the "New Laws," as they were known, but the laws stuck. Still, grave damage to the native population had already been done.

//////////////

Ecuadorian cacao was cheap because it was plentiful. But there was another reason for its low cost. When Indian labor dried up through disease and the new ban on the enslavement of indigenous Americans, the Spanish began importing slaves from

Africa, to whom the antislavery laws did not apply. This practice served a dual purpose: since the more bitter Forastero chocolate required large quantities of sugar to make it drinkable, the newly imported slaves could just as easily be put to work producing sugar on new plantations as they could be forced to gather and process cacao pods. It was a win-win for the plantation owners, and chocolate made from cheap cocoa and cheap sugar came, for the first time, within reach of everyone, from the wealthy to those of lesser means. Ecuador's Forastero cacao became known as "the cacao of the poor."

Ecuador's chief competitor in the lucrative new chocolate market was Venezuela. There, wild cacao called *Porcelana* grew on a narrow coastal plain along the edge of the Caribbean Sea. This variety was considered one of the purest examples of the finer Criollo type. Like the Ecuadorian Forastero, these trees had been growing wild in natural groves before the arrival of the Spaniards, though no one knows exactly when they first appeared there. The colonists eagerly began growing *Porcelana* trees on their own plantations in Venezuela. Here, too, the bustling international slave trade, carried out for three and a half centuries in what is known as the Middle Passage from West Africa across the Atlantic to America, provided the laborers. Spain wasn't alone in this practice; its major rivals France and Portugal also enthusiastically participated, along with England, Holland, and Denmark.

The way it worked was simple and effective from the point of view of those who benefited. In a "three-way trade" system, the slaving ships of a particular nation would carry manufactured goods such as clothing, weapons, and metal tools to African slave depots; these goods would be paid as barter for the human cargo of captured slaves, many obtained through the willing participation of other Africans. The slaves would be crammed into the holds of ships bound for

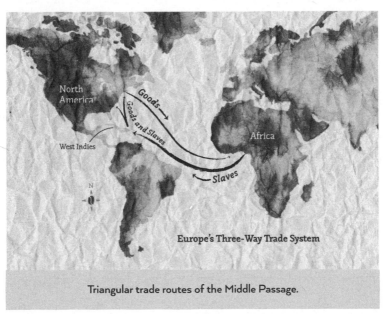

Triangular trade routes of the Middle Passage.

the sugar, cacao, indigo, and tobacco plantations of the Spanish colonies in the New World. Then the produce of those plantations would be brought back on the same ships and sold in the respective mother countries.

While the Spanish were establishing their cacao and sugar plantations and importing millions of African slaves to provide the labor, the Portuguese were ramping up their own cacao production. In Brazil, where wild Forastero cacao also grew, the Jesuit order of the Catholic Church initially controlled cocoa production. The priests would send native workers out into the forest on regular expeditions to collect wild cacao in large dugout canoes. This was extremely lucrative for the order, until smallpox and measles epidemics in the 1740s and 1750s decimated the population of Indian gatherers. By 1759, the Jesuits had been expelled from the colonies by the ruling heads of Portugal and Spain, and by the end of the nineteenth century the cacao plantations had all but disappeared from Brazil, owing to labor shortages, diseases of the cacao trees themselves, and the final abolishment of slavery in that country.

By then, cacao production had jumped continents again, to a place where wild cacao had never grown, and where only the hardier Forastero trees could survive. Beginning in 1824, the Portuguese transplanted Forastero cuttings from Brazil to Africa, initially to São Tomé in the Gulf of Guinea, then to Equatorial Guinea, and eventually to Ghana, Nigeria, and the Ivory Coast.

For the first time, it was not just chocolate that had traveled around the globe, but also the universal source—the cacao tree itself.

RECIPE

From *The American Physitian . . . Where-unto is Added a Discourse on the Cacao-Nut Tree, and the Use of Its Fruit, With All the Ways of Making Chocolate,* William Hughes, 1672.

"Take as many of the cacao's as you have a desire to make up at one time, and put as many of them at once into a frying-pan (being very clean scoured) as will cover the bottom thereof, and hold them over a moderate fire, shaking them so, that they may not burn (for you must have a very great care of that) until they are dry enough to peel off the outward crust skin; and after they are dried and peeled then beat them in an iron mortar, until it will rowl up into great balls or rows and be sure you beat it not over-much neither, for then it will become too much oyly."

CACAO VARIETALS?

Criollo, Forastero, or Trinitario. What's the difference? And how can you even know what kind has been used to make your chocolate bar? Like everything about chocolate, it's complicated.

Criollo is often described as delicate, low in "classic" chocolate flavor, but high in secondary, lingering flavor notes. So, what *is* classic chocolate flavor? It's hard to define, but words such as *bitter, roasted, fruity, earthy, woodsy,* and *nutty* are often enlisted to describe it. As with wines, chocolate connoisseurs may resort to comparing so-called classic flavors to substances that are not present in chocolate at all (grapefruit, fresh grass, ashes, or even tobacco!).

Whatever "classic" means, Forastero is a varietal typically strong in the classic chocolate flavor, but without the complex afternotes of Criollo (which might be called spicy or floral or even caramel-like, with a delicate natural sweetness unrelated to added sugar content). Some might call Forastero bitter while others would say it has a rich taste. Trinitario, a natural hybrid of Criollo and Forastero, is even harder to pin down; this varietal has an especially wide range of flavor profiles that derive from the mixed genetic heritage of particular Trinitario trees.

Despite all this variety, chocolate bars made from a blend of beans often don't carry that information on the label. Many bars are made from blends of several different Forastero beans, but Criollo beans are rarely blended with other types. Criollo cacao is rare, and its flavor is so delicate and subtle that it would be overpowered by stronger-flavored beans. Many chocophiles consider Criollo beans to be the highest quality of all, so it's likely, though not guaranteed, that the label on a bar made exclusively from Criollo beans will identify them.

In today's high-end chocolate bars, there's a whole new set of terms to figure out. For example, estate, or single-plantation, chocolate is made, as the name suggests, from cacao that is grown on one plantation. Chocolate makers grow it on their plantations and hold exclusive rights to the cacao that is produced from those operations.

In contrast, single-variety chocolate is made from one type of bean — Criollo, Forastero, or Trinitario. Some single-variety chocolate bars may also be of single origin, or even from a single farming estate. But the vast majority of chocolate bars are still made from a blend of beans.

None of these terms can tell you how *good* the chocolate is. The quality of chocolate depends not only on the flavor of the cacao beans, but also on proper processing of the raw material, as well as the skill of the chocolate maker.

What chocolate flavor is best? It's a matter of personal taste, but sampling different types is a good way to experience all the diversity that cacao has to offer.

Doing Well by Doing Good:
Chocolate in
the Industrial Age

*Caramels are just a fad. The chocolate
market will be a permanent one, because
it is more than just a sweet. It is a food.*

—Milton S. Hershey, in a conversation
with his cousin Frank Snavely, 1893

Despite its early origins in the Americas, it wasn't
until near the end of the nineteenth century, some
150 years after the Swedish botanist Carl Linnaeus
named the cacao tree and its fruit "food of the gods,"
that most people north of America's border with Mexico were introduced to the taste of chocolate.

It was different in Europe. Drinking chocolate had
swept the continent beginning in the seventeenth
century, and big changes in the ways in which cacao
beans were processed and consumed were under way
around the same time that North America was preoc-
cupied with its political revolution. It was in 1776 that
a Frenchman named Doret invented the hydraulic

A depiction of Carl Linnaeus.

press. This paved the way, in 1828, for a Dutch chemist and chocolate maker, Coenraad Van Houten, to invent his cocoa press, which he used to squeeze much of the cocoa butter from his beans.

The natural fat content of cocoa beans is about 52 percent, but Van Houten's press could reduce it by nearly half, leaving a dry cake that could be pulverized into a fine powder, called cocoa. Van Houten then added alkaline salts to make the cocoa powder mix more easily with water; the resulting beverage had a darker color, a milder taste, and a smoother consistency. The process became known as "dutching," and the product as "Dutch chocolate." Dutching not only changed the appearance, texture, and taste of chocolate; it also cut the price, and the added convenience and quality began, finally, to make chocolate into a drink for all Europeans, not just the wealthy elite. Dutching also led directly to the world's first chocolate bar, produced by J.S. Fry & Sons in England in 1874, since it made possible a chocolate substance that could be heated ("tempered") and then poured smoothly into molds, where it would cool and solidify. But it took almost another fifty years for a trio of Swiss innovators to complete the transformation of chocolate from bitter drink to sweet bar.

In 1875, after eight years of trial and error (undertaken only after he developed a crush on a local chocolate maker's daughter), Daniel Peter of Vevey, Switzerland, finally figured out how to combine milk and cocoa powder to make milk chocolate. The Swiss had been making chocolate since the middle of the nineteenth century, but there was a problem: they were mixing water with the chocolate, and water and chocolate didn't mix very well. The water caused chocolate to shrink, separate, and disintegrate, which explains the gritty consistency of drinking chocolate from the time of the ancient Mesoamericans. The Swiss had an abundance of cows, and it seemed to make sense that adding milk from local cows could result in a smoother chocolate. But milk, being 85 to 90 percent water, presented the same problem as water. Then Daniel Peter took his experiments to his neighbor, a pharmacist and food scientist named Henri Nestlé, who had for years been experimenting with various combinations of cow's milk, wheat flour, and sugar in hopes of developing an alternative source of infant nutrition for mothers who were unable to breastfeed their babies. Nestlé had already perfected the manufacture of condensed milk, composed of milk solids with much of the water removed; he and Peter soon thought up the idea of mixing sweetened condensed milk with cocoa powder, and milk chocolate was born. Nestlé and Peter kept the formula a closely guarded secret, and the product became an immediate sensation in Europe.

Four years later, in 1879, and less than fifty miles

from Vevey, in Berne, Rodolphe Lindt contributed his own major innovation to international chocolate making—the conching machine, so named because Lindt's original design was shaped like a conch shell. The machine heated and rolled a quantity of pressed chocolate for a prescribed number of hours, which produced a smoother, creamier chocolate that melted on the tongue; before Lindt invented his machine, even the finest eating chocolate had a grainy texture. Lindt also discovered that in the process of conching, he could add varying amounts of pure cocoa butter back to the mix to create even creamier forms of chocolate.

Meanwhile, a group of successful entrepreneurs in England was creating a new paradigm for chocolate. They wanted the chocolate they produced to be "ethical"—to embody quality and at the same time hold out the dual promise of health benefits and progressive social goals. For Quaker chocolatiers in England in the nineteenth century, chocolate became a means of doing well by doing good in the world.

The Quakers, more properly known as the Religious Society of Friends, had begun as a tiny minority movement of Protestant believers who had broken away from the established Church of England in the mid-seventeenth century. At the core of their beliefs lay the convictions that they could have a direct relationship with God and that all believers constituted a universal priesthood. In every act of their private lives, they strove to reflect an emotional purity that they believed came from "the light of God." They were persecuted as nonconformists and radicals. At the time of the Industrial Revolution, English Quakers were banned from attending universities and barred from most mainstream professions. Nor were they eligible to hold public office; among the few avenues open to them were business, commerce, and medicine. Many Quakers opened grocery shops, and some studied medicine through the apprenticeship system that was then the norm for physicians-in-training.

It was only natural, then, that chocolate, used for food, medicine, and religious sacrament through the centuries, would have held much appeal for enterprising English Quakers. In 1761, a Quaker physician in Bristol named Joseph Fry purchased an apothecary shop, where he was known to concoct a number of chocolate remedies he had devised. By 1847, his son had produced the world's first chocolate bar by grinding cocoa beans using the steam engine technology invented by James Watt, and then Van Houten's hydraulic press to extract liquid cocoa butter, which he then added back to the chocolate mix for greater viscosity. The finished chocolate was poured into molds to form solid bars.

In 1879, the same year in which Lindt invented his conching machine, another Quaker family, the Cadburys, moved their chocolate manufacturing plant from sooty, slum-infested Birmingham, England, to rural Bourneville in the West Midlands. There the Cadburys built a utopian company town for their workers that would later become an inspiration for Milton Hershey in Pennsylvania. The new factory in Bourneville was hailed at the time as a "factory in a garden."

The Cadbury business had begun in Birmingham as a one-man grocery shop that sold, among other goods, drinking chocolate and cocoa. It was opened in 1824 by John Cadbury, and the business grew steadily. John's brother and then his sons joined the enterprise. By then, the Frys, Cadburys, and at least two other Quaker families, the Rowntrees and the Terrys, had become synonymous with chocolate in England and remain so today. They chose chocolate for their family businesses for more reasons than taste alone, though. Their goals were ambitious. One of the most important was to persuade the poor to give up alcohol, which they felt led to violence and the destruction of families, in favor of the healthier chocolate drink. The Cadburys also campaigned to prevent the exploitation of young boys as chimney sweeps, and actively advanced animal welfare causes, adult education, and human rights. It was their policy to refuse to buy any cocoa beans that had been produced by means of slave labor. Officially abolished in the British Isles in 1833, slavery lingered, both officially and unofficially, in many locations where cacao was grown.

When Quakers promoted chocolate to the English public, they seemed to impart an elevated moral quality to what was then considered a strange and almost exotic food. Quakers had earned a reputation for honesty and reliability, and for selling goods that were free of the lead and brick dust that tainted so many food products of the time. They were among the first to set a firm price for their goods, marking each item at a consistent fair price to reassure buyers. Equality and justice ran through everything they did, and chocolate was a natural element in their quest to bring about social reform at a time when abuses ran rampant and protections for workers and consumers were few.

////////////

America's embrace of chocolate had begun before the U.S. Constitution created the structure for sustaining a new nation in 1787, but it was a quiet embrace. The first chocolate produced in the English colonies of North America appeared in 1765, when the Irish chocolate maker John Hanau and the Harvard-educated American doctor James Baker opened a processing house for cocoa beans in Dorchester, Massachusetts. They had imported the beans from the West Indies, and they turned them into solid cakes, which were then further refined by grinding them and mixing them with boiling water. But this early form of edible chocolate didn't become the sensation it had been in other parts of the world until European industrial advances made it convenient and pleasurable to eat chocolate as well as drink it.

Even into the early 1890s, the drinking chocolate that was all the rage across Europe was not widely consumed in most of America, and eating chocolate was unknown. It was other kinds of candy that Americans, especially American children, craved: butterscotches, sugar plums, lemon and peppermint drops, Gibraltars, sour candies, horehound, lavender and birch candy, and caramels.

That was about to change.

///////////////

COFFEE, TEA, OR COCOA?

Almost everyone has a favorite, and comparisons are often made among these three great nonalcoholic, plant-based hot drinks of the world. All three ancient beverages share certain components, notably caffeine, and all three produce physical and psychological effects, with nuances that are unique to each drink.

Stone Age peoples were familiar with most of the caffeine-producing plants. Early humans chewed the leaves, bark, and seeds of many plants because they enjoyed the sensations of alertness and elevated mood that some of these plants produced. Much later, people discovered that steeping these plants in hot water could release more of the natural stimulant, and from that realization came all of our present-day caffeinated drinks: coffee, tea, and cocoa (as well as cola, a relatively modern concoction invented by a pharmacist in Georgia in 1886).

Tea originated thousands of years ago in China and is enjoyed by more people than any other drink in the world. Before Dutch traders imported it into Europe in about 1610, it was mostly unknown to Westerners, many of whom routinely began their day with a mug of beer or ale. Made by simply steeping the cured leaves of the plant Camellia sinensis in boiling water, tea contains both caffeine and theobromine (common naturally occurring chemical compounds called alkaloids), but in considerably smaller amounts than are found in cocoa.

Coffee is a relative newcomer, dating to about the middle of the fifteenth century, where it was first grown and used in Ethiopia. It soon spread to Yemen and Egypt, and then into the rest of the Middle East, Persia, Turkey, and northern Africa. Brewed coffee contains a lot more caffeine than either tea or chocolate, but little, if any, theobromine. Like cocoa, it's made from the seeds of a fruit — the cherry of the shrublike Coffea plant — and similarly, these seeds are commonly called beans. In the process of making coffee, the cherries are harvested and the twin seeds within each fruit are removed, dried, roasted, and ground.

Taste is one of the reasons that these drinks have long been so popular all over the world. Another reason lies in their chemistry. Cacao seeds, the basis of both drinking and eating chocolate, contain small and varying amounts of caffeine, but considerably more theobromine than either tea or coffee. Like caffeine, theobro-

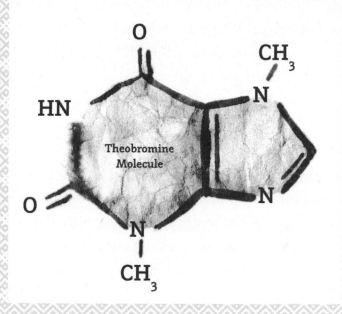

O

HN

CH₃

N

Theobromine
Molecule

O

N

N

CH₃

mine belongs to the class of alkaloid molecules known as methylxanthines. These molecules naturally occur in as many as sixty different plant species. Caffeine is the primary methlyxanthine in coffee, and theophylline is the primary methylxanthine in tea. Theobromine, which is present in both drinking and eating chocolate, is the primary methylxanthine found in products of the tree that bears its name, *Theobroma cacao*. Though all these methylxanthines are closely related, their effects are subtly different. In general, caffeine has been shown to have a greater stimulant effect on the human nervous system than theobromine, but theobromine may have a greater beneficial effect on mood.

One fall day in 1893, Milton Snavely Hershey stood with his cousin Frank Snavely in a cavernous, noisy hall at the huge World's Columbian Exposition in Chicago. The soft-spoken, thirty-six-year-old Hershey, a Pennsylvania farm boy by birth, had been spending most of an extended trip to Chicago surrounded by the gleaming, white marble city within a city that had been constructed to commemorate the four hundredth anniversary of Columbus's arrival in America. At the heart of this great world's fair, which lasted for six months and occupied more than six hundred acres, was a large reflecting pool that represented the long voyage Columbus undertook to the New World. It was clearly meant to dazzle.

Milton Hershey, though he'd endured a difficult childhood and early adulthood, was by this time a wealthy, self-made man who had seen much of the world with his own eyes. What interested him most that day was not the opulence of the setting or the crowds of visitors from all over the globe who milled about, testing and tasting new products and wares, riding on the prototype Ferris wheel, or enjoying Buffalo Bill's famous Wild West Show. What drew Hershey most irresistibly was the Palace of Mechanic Arts, and in particular, a display of industrial equipment by J. M. L›mann of Dresden, Germany.

A southern view of the Palace of Mechanic Arts at the World's Columbian Exposition of 1893, more commonly known as the Chicago World's Fair.

The German company had erected a small factory that was busy transforming raw cacao beans into chocolate bars in full view of visitors. Hershey and his cousin stood transfixed; they inhaled the intoxicating aroma of the roasting cocoa and observed the grinding, mixing, rolling, and molding that turned one thing into something entirely different and unexpected.

Hershey had sampled Swiss milk chocolate on one of his European tours. He had a hunch it would appeal to the American palate. He'd also toured the

Milton S. Hershey in 1887, at age thirty.

Cadburys' utopian factory town of Bourneville, which left an indelible impression on the idealistic, progressive Hershey. His European travels had been scouting trips as much as recreation; he was always looking for ideas that he could mold to his own purposes back home in Pennsylvania. And from the time he'd seen what the Swiss chemists and English Quaker activists were doing with chocolate, a big idea had begun to form in his mind.

Hershey felt a certain kinship with the English Quakers. To escape persecution in England, thousands of Quakers had migrated to America and settled in the colony of Pennsylvania, which was founded in 1682 by their countryman William Penn. Following this same trajectory were Milton Hershey's Swiss ancestors, who arrived in Pennsylvania in the early 1700s. The Hershey family was Mennonite, not Quaker, but the two groups had important things in common: they both had suffered persecution as nonconformists and outsiders; both held pacifist and antislavery convictions and believed in hard work; and members of both groups espoused a belief in ethical thinking and principled b›avior in all aspects of their lives. Milton Hershey's parents both had been raised in a conservative Mennonite tradition and each, in a way, had left that tradition or moved beyond it. But there was a strain of freethinking radicalism within the extremely conservative Reformed Mennonite Church in Pennsylvania; in the case of Milton's troubled family, the church may not have been as central an influence as it had been for his grandparents, but the basic beliefs of their Mennonite tradition played out in all of their lives in unpredictable ways, including the influence of the Quaker chocolate makers on Milton Hershey. In later life, when asked what his religion was, Hershey often replied, simply, "The golden rule."

Faith was a backdrop, but apparently not a driving force, in his life. Milton's mother came from a prosperous farming family. She was practical, the daughter of a frugal church bishop. She was accustomed to a comfortable but conservative lifestyle. Milton's father was a dreamer with little education but plenty of big ideas that never panned out. He had little use for either the church or the farming life. In Milton's early years, his family moved from place to place as his father chased after various business schemes that failed. He attended at least seven schools but never progressed past the fourth grade. By the time he was twelve, his beloved little sister had died of scarlet fever and his parents' always difficult marriage was over. Though his father would reappear in his life from time to time — usually with some ill-advised business counsel that did more harm than good — the family was broken.

Milton was no stranger to the candy trade. His mother found him his first real job with a sweets maker in Lancaster, Pennsylvania, when he was just fifteen. He had failed miserably in a brief stint as a printer's apprentice, a position arranged by his father, who hoped his son would become a man of letters.

Making candy was more to Milton's liking, and by the age of nineteen, he had launched his own business, M. S. Hershey's Spring Garden Confectionery Works. The fledgling company debuted at a smaller-scale forerunner of the World's Columbian Exposition—Philadelphia's 1876 Centennial Exposition. Milton's soft, chewy caramels made with milk were an instant hit, but this early success fizzled out, as did several later attempts to start candy businesses in Denver, Chicago, and New York City. It looked as if Milton might be following in his father's footsteps after all.

It wasn't until Milton came up with a new formula for his caramels — he added more milk to create a creamy candy that wouldn't stick to the teeth — that the then twenty-eight-year-old entrepreneur found lasting success. His Lancaster Caramel Company took off, and in just a few years it had made him wealthier than he'd ever imagined he could become. His growing fortune soon allowed him to dream even bigger dreams, and to hope for a future that would make up for his father's failures.

Though Milton Hershey was always personally involved in every aspect of his business ventures, and especially enjoyed tinkering with new recipes and ingredients, business was of limited interest to him once his caramel company had succeeded beyond his and his mother's wildest dreams. His newfound wealth fueled a restless penchant for travel, and for even bigger dreams.

"I have more money than I know what to do with," he sometimes said when advisors suggested ways in which his company could become larger and more profitable. His father's son in one way, he still wanted more, but not necessarily more wealth. He wanted to do something important in the world.

He wasn't sure what he was looking for, but when he saw freshly made chocolate bars that day in Chicago, he knew he'd found it. Never one to agonize over a decision, he bought all of the J. M. L›mann equipment on the spot and arranged for it to be boxed up at the close of the exposition and shipped to his factory in Lancaster. He would sell his caramel company and stake his future on chocolate. With cutting-edge European machinery in his possession and his talent for divining the tastes of Americans, he would apply himself to the challenge of transforming chocolate from the gritty, bitter, handmade drink of the Mesoamericans into a triumph of the industrial age. He would make his own "great American chocolate bar."

By the time Hershey made his fateful decision, another Pennsylvania candy maker had begun to market a chocolate candy called Wilbur Buds — a forerunner of Hershey's famous Kiss, as it turned out. Wilbur Buds were manufactured in Lititz, Pennsylvania, just a few miles from Milton Hershey's Lancaster Caramel Company and from the site of his next plant: his birthplace of Derry Church, Pennsylvania, soon to be renamed Hershey. Perhaps Milton — or M.S., as he was then called by his loyal workers — was thinking of Wilbur Buds that day at the Chicago exposition when he decided to enter the chocolate business. Later in 1893, money in hand from the sale of his caramel business, he started to build the world's largest chocolate manufacturing plant in Derry Church. It was a remote, pastoral setting, surrounded by dairy farms to provide a ready supply of milk for his chocolate and close to rail lines ready to ship it.

The Hershey Chocolate Company factory opened in 1905, but Milton Hershey had bigger plans. He had decided to build an entire town for his workers, modeled on Quaker company towns such as Cadbury's Bourneville in the English countryside.

He hired an architect to create the town grid, and began laying trolley lines and building modern homes on tree-lined streets with names like Chocolate Avenue and Cocoa Avenue. Unlike most homes in America at the time, the homes that Milton Hershey would build would all have electricity, indoor plumbing, and central heating. He would provide every amenity: a public library, a gymnasium, golf courses, and a 150-acre park with a band shell, a zoo, and an expansive swimming pool. All this would be subsidized by his chocolate company, which meant that property taxes would be half what they were in most American cities. There would be provisions for local government, but no police department or jail. As one New York business writer gushed, having seen the plans for the place he called Chocolate Town, "These are not expected to be necessary under the conditions. Incarceration and punishment are for criminals—unhappy mortals. Here there will be no unhappiness, then why any crime?"

There was just one problem. Hershey's utopian plan was built around the idea of marketing milk chocolate, like the kind he'd tasted in Switzerland during his frequent travels abroad. No one in America was making it, and Hershey was sure it would catch on in a big way, but the secret of Swiss milk chocolate remained with the Swiss. Hershey had tried many recipes, but hadn't yet perfected a process for mass-producing deliciously sweet milk chocolate that also had a satisfactory shelf life. Though plain dark chocolate and so-called Dutch cocoa kept indefinitely, the milk chocolate he was already selling locally quickly turned rancid, placing limits on how far it could be shipped. The problem centered on the very ingredient that defined his product: the milk.

With his factory walls going up, Hershey was in a race against time to perfect his product. With his handpicked research team, he retreated to the family homestead at Derry Church, where they experimented b>ind closed doors, in the utmost secrecy, for sixteen hours a day. Finally, frustrated and running out of time, Hershey hired a chemist; when the man's efforts resulted in a burned batch of milk and sugar, Hershey dismissed him and brought in a trusted employee from his Lancaster plant. John Schmalbach and M. S. Hershey went alone to the private laboratory Hershey had set up, outfitted with huge copper vacuum kettles in his own creamery, using fresh, naturally lower-fat milk from his own herd of Holsteins.

The breakthrough came when Schmalbach started with skim milk, to which he added a large quantity of sugar. He gently heated the mixture at a low temperature for several hours, evaporating the water content, then let it cool. The result was warm, smooth sweetened condensed milk that took to cocoa powder, cocoa butter, and other ingredients without getting lumpy. It was the discovery that made all the difference.

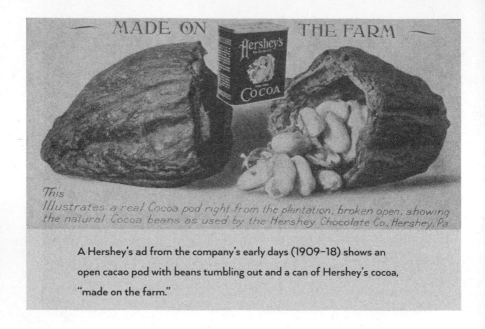

— MADE ON THE FARM —

This illustrates a real Cocoa pod right from the plantation, broken open, showing the natural Cocoa beans as used by the Hershey Chocolate Co., Hershey, Pa.

A Hershey's ad from the company's early days (1909–18) shows an open cacao pod with beans tumbling out and a can of Hershey's cocoa, "made on the farm."

Hershey's milk chocolate never did taste just like Swiss chocolate. The liquid condensed milk fermented slightly in the manufacturing process, giving the product a faint sour note under the sweetness that was absent from Swiss milk chocolate, which was made from powdered condensed milk. Americans quickly learned to love Hershey's milk chocolate, even though Europeans found it slightly off-putting. When the plant opened in June 1905, the five-cent Hershey's milk chocolate bar became an instant success. Finally, there was affordable, mass-produced chocolate for everyone in the United States! In the factory's first year, net sales of Hershey's chocolate topped $1 million.

Milton Hershey went on to build a stately mansion in the town for himself and his adored wife, Catherine (Kitty). They had married in 1898, when he was forty-two and she was twenty-six. When they were unable to have children, he established a residential school for orphan boys on a hill overlooking his town — a decision perhaps influenced by his own lack of educational stability as a boy. Years before his death, he secretly placed all of the Hershey Chocolate Company's stock, worth more than $60 million at the time, into a trust to benefit the school, which is today a coed boarding school that serves eighteen hundred students from disadvantaged backgrounds. With over $6 billion in assets, it is one of the wealthiest schools in the world.

Milton Hershey died a voluntary pauper in 1945, after a long career that would include replicating his Hershey utopia in Cuba. There he established sugar plantations, factories, and a railway, and founded Central Hershey, another company town, near Havana. He provided many amenities for his employees, as he had in his U.S. utopian town: health care, free public schools that had been lacking there before, baseball diamonds, and golf courses. The Hershey

Chocolate Company survived a world sugar crisis in 1921 and the Great Depression of the 1930s, when employment in "his" town kept humming along, with little disruption. It continued to prosper during World War II, when Hershey's chocolate became a staple of U.S. troops' rations — a continuation of the military's embrace of American chocolate that had begun in the First World War.

It's to the requirements of military field service that we owe products such as Mars, Inc.'s M&M's, "the candy that melts in your mouth, not in your hand!" M&M's were the result of a collaboration between Hershey's and Mars that occurred during a brief kinder, gentler time in the business of Big Candy. Since World War II, chocolate candy has been in continuous huge demand in the United States, with Hershey's main competitor, Mars, rising to share the wealth generated by a seemingly insatiable American desire for affordable chocolate.

///////////////

In Hershey, Pennsylvania, many things have changed since its founding as Chocolate Town, U.S.A. Now it's a bustling community of more than fourteen thousand, known as much for its major medical center and Disney-like theme park as for its rich (in more ways than one) history. But Hershey's is still the largest chocolate company in North America. It still makes milk chocolate according to the original 1905 formula, in a town where the streetlights are replicas of

the iconic Hershey's Kiss, and anytime, day or night, the air is rich with the fragrance of roasting cocoa.

RECIPE

Chocolate Custards

From the popular magazine *Godey's Lady's Book*, 1854.

Dissolve gently by the side of the fire an ounce and a half of the best chocolate in rather more than a wineglassful of water, and then boil it until it is perfectly smooth; mix with it a pint of milk well flavored with lemon-peel or vanilla, and two ounces of fine sugar, and when the whole boils, stir into it five well-beaten eggs that have been strained. Put the custard into a jar or jug, set it into a pan of boiling water, and stir it without ceasing until it is thick. Do not put it into glasses or a dish till nearly or quite cold. These, as well as other custards, are infinitely finer when made with the yolks only of the eggs.

The Dark Side
of Chocolate

*The leading British cocoa firms, as we
have shown, are awake, or are
awakening, to their responsibilities. It
remains for the British public, and we trust
also for the public of the United States,
to play their part. They must not let the
whole brunt of the battle fall upon the
manufacturers. They must let it be known
that if needs be they will stand loyally by
any and every firm which refuses
to use slave-grown cocoa.*

—*The Spectator,* December 12, 1908, London

There has always been a dark side to chocolate, and
it has nothing to do with whether or not there's milk
and sugar in the recipe. That dark side is human slavery, and though it has not always been called that,
it's a stain that has followed chocolate throughout its
long history. From the first, chocolate production and
consumption have been all about inequalities. Ancient Mesoamerican cultures had their own servant

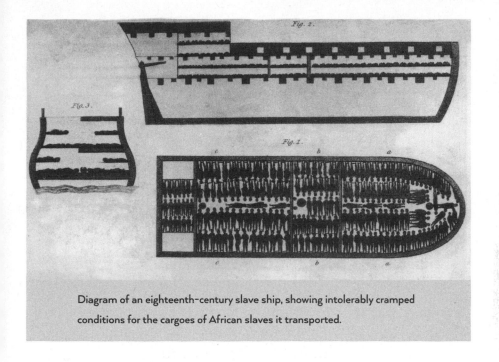

Diagram of an eighteenth-century slave ship, showing intolerably cramped conditions for the cargoes of African slaves it transported.

classes that catered to elite warriors and rulers; these servants were responsible for harvesting and preparing the chocolate drink, but were rarely if ever permitted to enjoy it. Exploitation cut across cultures; long before the first European set foot on American shores, the more powerful members of native societies had been enslaving the unlucky and weaker among them simply because they could, because it was accepted, and because they received many benefits from slave labor.

After Cortés, Pizarro, and other conquistadors conquered the original populations of Central and South America, one of the first things they did was to enslave the Mesoamericans who survived the violence and disease that had been brought to their lands. A few of the indigenous people were able to resist, but most were subjugated by the overwhelming power of the conquerors.

After colonizing the populations they had defeated, the Spaniards quickly established cacao plantations throughout growing regions of Central and South America; by 1810 their trees in Venezuela produced half of all the world's cacao. At the same time, as they came to understand that cacao would grow anywhere along the equator with adequate shade, moisture, and other essentials, the colonists began transplanting it to other islands they controlled throughout the Caribbean and in the Philippines. Other European colonial powers—the Dutch, English, French, and Portuguese—soon followed suit, introducing cacao into Indonesia, Curaçao, Ceylon (now called Sri Lanka), Jamaica, Martinique, St. Lucia, the Dominican Republic, Brazil, the Guianas, and Madagascar throughout the 1600s.

The Portuguese, who had already claimed Brazil, began extensive cacao cultivation there, too, then started plantations on the small islands of Principe and São Tomé, just off the west coast of Africa. Not to be outdone, Spain established plantings on the nearby island of Fernando Po (now called Bioko). Attempts by the Dutch (in 1815) and the Swiss (in 1853) to start cacao plantations on the mainland of Africa had failed, but beginning in 1879, a trained blacksmith and agriculturalist named Tetteh Quarshie, a native of Africa's Gold Coast (present-day Ghana), succeeded in smuggling seedlings from Fernando Po across the Gulf of Guinea. He became the Johnny Cocoa-seed of Africa. The cacao trees he planted in Gold Coast eventually spread into French-held territory along the Ivory Coast and into Nigeria. By 1920, the trees that Quarshie had planted matured. They began producing fruit at the same time that disease and environmental degradation were causing a near collapse of cacao groves in the Americas. West Africa thus became the world's leading exporter of cacao.

////////////

Within a few years of the Spanish conquest, slaves were imported from Africa to work not only in the new cacao groves, but also in the colonial sugar and cotton fields of the Caribbean and the Americas. The need for labor seemed limitless, and as world de-

This illustration of slaves captured in Africa appeared in Germany in the 1875 edition of *Systematic Illustrated Atlas of the Conversations-Lexicon, Iconographic Encyclopedia of Sciences and the Arts,* published by Brockhaus Verlaghaus.

mand for chocolate continued to grow, more and more slaves were needed to keep up the pace of production. Landowners, traders, and merchants all benefited as chocolate became more affordable, and thus more popular.

In the fashionable gentlemen's chocolate houses of London during the seventeenth and eighteenth centuries, intellectuals and philosophers debated the rights of kings, the role of the Church, and the potential for improvement of the common man's lot while sipping sugar-sweetened chocolate and coffee produced by the blood and sweat of slaves half a world away.

By the mid-1800s, after 250 years of human misery, the slave trade was outlawed throughout Europe; in the United States it would take a few more years and a bloody civil war to accomplish this. But unofficially, in hot, tropical places on the margins of society, people still lived and died in slavery. Now they were called by new names: indentured laborers, contract workers, or *servicais*. Officially, these laborers were promised jobs and wages in the cocoa groves of colonial plantations. They were told that they could work for a time and then return home anytime they chose with the money they'd earned. In reality, most were forced to work indefinitely, and there was no way to return home.

This was the situation on the Portuguese-controlled islands of São Tomé and Principe, 150 miles off the west coast of Africa, at the start of the twentieth century. Here the cacao crop was produced by forty thousand slaves; it was also here, from 1901 to 1908, that the reform-minded, Quaker-owned Cadbury Company of England had been purchasing half of all the beans used in making their chocolate products. In the early years of the century, articles began to appear in the British press suggesting that Cadbury was violating its own ideals and standards in purchasing cocoa beans from São Tomé in the face of mounting evidence that this and other Portuguese-run plantations were using slave labor.

The Cadburys were, after all, members of the British and Foreign Anti-Slavery Society and other progressive organizations. By 1909, it had been eight years, at least, since Portugal's state-sanctioned use of slave labor (called by another name) had come to international light and had been subject to vocal criticism. Yet the Cadbury family continued to do business there, claiming that discreet diplomacy, along with uninterrupted purchase of São Tomé's cacao, would do more to improve the workers' lives than a boycott would. In the meantime, as many as six thousand slaves died on the island each year that business as usual continued. Pressure from humanitarian groups was equally ineffective in persuading the Portuguese to stop the practice of slavery.

The scandal came to a head with a libel suit filed by Cadbury Brothers Limited against the *London Standard* newspaper, which had run an editorial that was highly critical of the company's policy with regard to its cocoa sourcing. The case was argued in a high-profile trial in 1909. In the end, Cadbury technically won its case, but the award of only a token amount for damages was considered a victory by the defense and a vindication of the charge that Cadbury had turned a blind eye to slavery in the production of its cocoa. By then, Cadbury had already acted to change its policies, even enlisting fellow Quaker chocolate makers Fry and Rowntree to change theirs as well. William Cadbury took his antislavery case to the highest levels of the British government, an act that inflamed tensions between the now antislavery Britain and Portugal, which still embraced the practice. It also highlighted how the practice of forced labor still persisted a full century after legal abolition of the slave trade.

Slowly, reforms were put into place. But it was only with the end of colonialism, as one by one the countries of West Africa gained their independence, that many of the worst abuses began to be addressed by the new African governments. It wasn't until 1975 that Portugal gave up its control of Angola, São Tomé, and Principe and the policy of forced labor there was officially abolished. As abolitionist sympathy gained popularity in the major chocolate-consuming countries, chocolate makers stopped buying beans from the Portuguese islands, just as a new cacao industry found its footing in Ghana. There the industry developed on a small local scale, with family farms largely avoiding the use of forced migrant labor. This made buying beans from Ghana more attractive to chocolate companies, their shar›olders, and consumers.

MAKING THE CONNECTION

Chocolate is a unique food that defies the growing locavore trend. A locavore is someone who tries, as much as possible, to eat foods that are produced locally, rather than foods that are moved long distances to markets. This practice can be good for consumers and for the planet. But to do this with chocolate, you'd have to live very near the equator, where the raw materials of chocolate — cocoa beans — are produced, and even if you did, you'd have a hard time finding much chocolate to eat. That's because chocolate and cocoa powder — the food products that are made from the cacao fruit — are manufactured and sold, for the most part, in an entirely different part of the world from where cocoa beans are produced — primarily in Europe and North America. There are many reasons for this, including chocolate's relatively low melting point, which not only causes it to "melt in your mouth," but which also makes working with it in cooler climates much easier.

Americans today consume more than 3 billion pounds of chocolate a year. But Europeans eat even more of it, and worldwide consumption totals 3 million tons per year. Yet in West Africa, which now supplies nearly 70 percent of the world's cocoa beans, eating chocolate is practically unknown; all of Africa accounts for just 3 percent of world consumption. It's this disconnect between production and consumption of chocolate, ever since the secret of chocolate first crossed the ocean to Europe and back again to North America, that has long fueled poverty, slavery, and human exploitation in the cocoa-producing regions of the world.

//////////////

Slavery in the production of cocoa beans has not gone away. Most people would be horrified to know that the chocolate bar they unwrap today may have been made with cocoa beans supplied by the hard, dangerous, and sometimes brutally enforced labor of children as young as seven or eight, in some of the poorest countries on the planet. The most persistent of these labor practices occur in the nations of West Africa. Ivory Coast (Côte d'Ivoire), today the world's leading supplier of cocoa beans, employs more than 109,000 children in its cocoa industry, who work under "the worst forms of child labor," according to a report published by the U.S. Department of State. The same government report concludes that some 10,000 of these children are victims of human trafficking or enslavement. They are robbed not only of their freedom and their childhood, but of their right to a basic education, which might allow them to break the cycle of extreme poverty into which they've been born.

Most people agree that the root causes of persistent modern-day child slavery in the cocoa industry are twofold: poverty at the bottom of the production ladder, and a quest for ever higher profit margins at the top. While the global chocolate market—80 percent of which is controlled by just six large transnational corporations, including household names such as Mars, Nestlé, and Hershey—generates nearly $100 billion per year, small growers in impoverished countries like Ivory Coast and Ghana receive only a few pennies of each of those dollars. Often, out of desperation, these small cocoa farmers turn to cheap labor—even slave labor—from children even more desperate to survive.

At the same time, some observers suggest that the cocoa business and West African society are too complex to yield simple answers to this problem. According to Órla Ryan, author of the 2012 book *Chocolate*

Nations: Living and Dying for Cocoa in West Africa, it's not always easy to tell whether chocolate workers in Ghana and Ivory Coast are really slaves or just laborers who farm cacao because they're desperately poor and can't get better-paying work. And while it's true that some of these scarcely paid laborers are children, many of their impoverished parents are grateful that their children have found work, believing that they will be fed and sheltered—and may be able to save enough money to eventually attend school. Most of the children stopped at the border between Ghana and Ivory Coast are reportedly glad to be leaving home and getting work, likely because they don't understand what awaits them as workers in the cocoa industry. Many other children doing this hard work are the offspring and extended family of growers. "In this kind of hand-to-mouth existence," says Ryan, "family labor holds cocoa enterprises together. Without it, smallholders would struggle to harvest the crop."

But still, it's a known fact that thousands of children are kidnapped or sold into slavery, taken across borders, and forced to perform dangerous, grueling labor at little or no pay—a reality largely hidden from privileged consumers in other parts of the world, who are for the most part unaware that they are enjoying a candy bar that child laborers in West Africa will never taste. Meanwhile, the profits of the international chocolate industry continue to soar. Breaking this cycle will require direct action on the part of the major chocolate companies—a willingness to pay more for their beans, and a commitment to work toward ending the practice of child slavery in some of the countries where companies purchase the beans. Consumers will also need to play a part, by demanding that chocolate companies eliminate slave labor from their supply chains and by being willing to pay a bit more for chocolate that is made without slave labor.

///////////////

As in the case last century of *Cadbury v. The London Standard*, public pressure and media attention today have begun to make a difference, but the pace of change is slow. In 2001, in an attempt to avoid intense negative publicity and new government regulations, many of the major chocolate companies (including Hershey, Mars, and Nestlé) signed an agreement known as the Harkin-Engel Protocol, referred to sometimes as the Cocoa Protocol, pledging to certify their cocoa "child labor free" by 2005. Unfortunately, the companies failed to comply, so the deadline was extended to 2008. But still the companies continued

A young boy weeds beneath trees on his father's cacao farm in Ghana. The Fair Trade cooperative to which his father belongs helped bring fresh water and a better school for the children of impoverished cacao farmers, along with higher prices for the farmers' cocoa beans.

to purchase cocoa from countries known to employ forced child labor, and the deadline was extended yet again, to 2010.

Since then, some of the biggest companies have finally taken concrete first steps to comply with the *new* new deadline. Hershey, America's largest chocolate producer, whose founder built his reputation on a commitment to children, consumers, and community, was the last major company to comply. Pressure from advocacy groups and consumers, and even from some of the company's own shar>olders, eventually led to a major new commitment from Hershey in late 2012. The company pledged then that all of its chocolate products will be made from 100 percent certified cacao beans by the year 2020.

So what is certified cacao? Certification is a tool that was developed to help ensure that cacao and other commodities such as coffee are produced sustainably, safely, and efficiently. Several certification organizations like Fair Trade, the Rainforest Alliance, and UTZ Certified have developed advanced standards for organizing, training, and auditing cacao farmers. Through certification, farmers benefit from comprehensive training programs via third-party organizations and are checked by independent auditors. One of the things the auditors try to monitor is whether child slavery is present in the operation of a cacao farm. Of the certifying organizations, Fair Trade is the best known and is widely considered to be the most effective in identifying and discouraging the use of child slavery on small, scattered farms in remote locations.

Fair Trade certifiers are international federations that coordinate, promote, and facilitate the work of Fair Trade organizations. Certification is designed to be a

Look for the Fair Trade U.S.A. or Fair Trade International logo when purchasing chocolate.

mutually beneficial process. It gives farmers a better organizational structure within which to work and improved access to markets to help them build successful farms and increase their income. In turn, companies that partner with certifying organizations receive a traceable, safe supply of high-quality, sustainably produced cocoa. By displaying the certifying logo on their chocolate bars and other products, these companies will attract one of the fastest-growing segments of the chocolate market — those who are concerned with where their food originates and whether it's produced responsibly and humanely.

In theory, farmers who join certified collectives

such as Fair Trade are guaranteed a minimum price for their cocoa beans, besides having their farms monitored for sustainable growing practices and for the absence of slave labor. But in practice, though it's a big step in the right direction, it's an imperfect system. Fair Trade initiatives lack the resources to police every small farm that signs on, and Fair Trade buyers may not always pay more to the farmers than private buyers would pay.

Some small cacao farmers are more concerned with being paid a fair price up front, when the cocoa beans change hands, than they are in possibly being paid slightly more later, after their product has passed through the steps of certifying agencies and middlemen. Some growers are so poor that they don't have the luxury of waiting for the more complex certifying process to unfold.

But Fair Trade and the other certifying organizations aren't the only solution. A few innovative, smaller companies are developing new ways of dealing directly and fairly with growers who produce the cocoa beans they use to make their chocolate. This means more than just paying a fair price for the beans so that farmers can pay their workers a living wage. It means investing in the community where the cacao is grown, helping to raise the standard of living —

including health care and education — for families who still struggle.

Public involvement, as always, drives change; the children's chocolate strike of 1947 was part of a long, honorable, and often successful tradition that continues to bring about important reforms in the chocolate industry in the twenty-first century.

///////////////

The family of cacao producer and Fair Trade cooperative member Miguel Rivera (left), forty-two; his wife, Lilliana Alvardo Lopez, thirty-nine; and their daughter, Alejandra, four. They live and work near Piura, northwestern Peru.

For most people on earth, eating chocolate feels like a necessity, almost like breathing air and drinking water. But for the estimated 5 million hous›olds that farm cacao as a cash crop, it is literally a necessity of life. Their survival depends on it. Chocolate is a glue that binds people, cultures, history, and the health of the planet. It's a bridge to understanding. Crossing that bridge presents many barricades built on centuries of oppression, exploitation, and misunderstanding, and it has been a long road to try to reach this understanding, and we're not all the way there yet. But luckily, we have chocolate to sustain us on the journey!

In a remote river canyon in Peru, cacao pods in various stages of ripeness hang like bright lanterns in the midday sun.

Yaritza Barberan, age five, eats delicious pulp from a recently harvested cacao pod in Ecuador.

A llama gazes serenely near the ancient Inca capital then known as Qosquo.

Painting of Christopher Columbus landing in the West Indies on October 12, 1492, on an island that the natives called Guanahani and he named San Salvador.

From the sixteenth-century manuscript "History of the Indians" (1579) by Diego Duran, Cortés being welcomed by Indians to the beating of drums.

After his beheading by the Lords of the Death, Hun Hunaphu's head is hung in a cacao tree. Maya drawing from a ceramic vessel found in Guatemala.

Portrait of Motecuhzoma II (1466–1520), last Aztec king at Tenochtitlan, Mexico. Engraving by A. Delvaux, 1832.

Feathered serpent head in Templo Mayor, Tenochtitlán, Mexico City.

The pathogenic fungi that cause witches' broom on cacao tree limbs also attack the pods, destroying the beans inside.

Not all fungi that infect cacao trees are ugly; some are beautiful, but still deadly. Spores released from the fan-shaped fruit of this inch-wide *Crinipellis perniciosa* mushroom can infect trees, causing witches' broom, which drastically reduces yields.

Don Fortunato on his farm high in the Marañón canyon, surrounded by a mixed profusion of his crops.

The Marañón River may be crossed by boat or barge, depending on river conditions.

Noe displays a freshly opened pod.

White beans!

Brian Horsley looks over a pile of colorful cacao pods, newly harvested and waiting to be opened.

Cacao grows best in lush rainforest environments.

An aerial view of Amazonia, a portion of the Amazon rainforest in Brazil.

Fortunato No. 4 chocolate, a "fine-flavor" treat made from Pure Nacional cacao, identified after its discovery by the American entrepreneurs Dan Pearson and Brian Horsley in northern Peru.

Grandma Crowell's fudge pie.

Scenes from the Peruvian rainforest (on this page and the following page), cacao's place of origin and center of diversity.

RECIPE

Toll House Chocolate Crunch Cookie

From *Toll House Tried and True Recipes*,
Ruth Graves Wakefield, 1936.

2¼ cups all-purpose flour
1 teaspoon baking soda
1 teaspoon salt
1 cup butter, softened
¾ cup granulated sugar
¾ cup packed brown sugar
1 teaspoon vanilla extract
2 eggs
2 cups semisweet chocolate morsels
1 cup chopped nuts

❖ Combine flour, baking soda, and salt in a small bowl. Beat butter, granulated sugar, brown sugar, and vanilla in large mixer bowl. Add eggs one at a time, beating well after each addition; gradually beat in flour mixture. Stir in morsels and nuts. Drop by rounded tablespoon onto ungreased baking sheets.

❖ Bake in preheated 375-degree Fahrenheit (191 degrees Celcius) oven for 9 to 11 minutes or until golden brown. Let stand for 2 minutes; remove to wire racks to cool completely.

Candy, Food,
or Medicine?

*The persons who habitually take chocolate
are those who enjoy the most equable
and constant health and are least liable
to a multitude of illnesses which
spoil the enjoyment of life.*

—Jean Anthelme Brillat-Savarin, *The Physiology of Taste*, 1825

When you hear the word *chocolate*, you probably think of a rectangular candy bar—dark or milk chocolate, with nuts or without, sweet and rich. But for most of its very long history, chocolate was not a candy. It was first used as a drink that was thought to be more nourishing than most foods, and it was also used as a medicine in which people invested the power to heal a wide range of ailments. From the very beginning, this versatile substance has filled a dual, sometimes confusing, role as both medicine and food.

While Mesoamericans incorporated elements of magic into their healing arts, their practical medical understanding was far ahead of the Europeans', thanks to their extensive botanical knowledge. They understood the actions of hundreds of plants that grew around them—plants that often brought about real cures. The Aztec emperor even kept a botanical garden in which many plants were grown and tested. Cacao-based treatments had a central place in Meso-american medicine. They were commonly given as a remedy for stomach disorders, diarrhea, coughs, and fatigue. In various forms, cacao was used to treat rashes, fevers, and seizures. Mixed with the bark of the silk cotton tree (*Castilla elastica*), it was helpful in fighting generalized infections. Combined with the heart flower (*Talauma mexicana*), it was employed to treat cardiac disorders. It was taken as a soothing agent; an antiseptic; a stimulant; a remedy for snake-bites, sterility, and menstrual troubles; and for basic sustenance and weight gain. A poultice made from the flower of the cacao tree was used to treat injured or sore feet. No part of the plant was wasted. Even its broad, waxy leaves could be ground up and used as a diuretic and to treat burns.

The conquistadors who first learned of chocolate in Mesoamerica were repulsed by its use in the blood rituals of the Aztecs and perplexed by the natives' fondness for drinking the bitter brew. "A drink more fit for pigs!" one exclaimed. But the Spanish were deeply fascinated with the idea of medicinal uses for chocolate.

According to the Maya scholar and chocolate historian Michael D. Coe, the Spanish invaders were obsessed with matters of the body. This preoccupation makes a kind of sense, given the state of Western medicine at the time, which was based almost entirely on classical Grefi theories that dated back

A plaster bust of Hippocrates, often called the father of Western medicine.

to Hippocrates (460–377 B.C.) and Galen (ca. A.D. 131–201).

The core principle of these teachings, called "humorism," proposed that all disease is caused by imbalances within the natural order, or "temperament," of the body. The basic elements of life — air, earth, fire, and water — were thought to be linked to four "humors" that were contained in various proportions within the human body. These were blood, black bile, phlegm, and yellow bile. The balance of these universal humors could be upset, and with dire consequences. One or more could be depleted by inhaling or absorbing through the skin certain "vapors," but humors were also affected by diet and activity. Each humor was understood to be either wet or dry, and hot or cold — though how this was determined is unclear.

On the basis of whichever humor was thought to predominate in a person, doctors advised treating the person's symptoms with a medicine or food that had the opposite quality, to restore balance. A "hot" fever called for a "cold" drug, but whether the patient was predominantly of a wet or dry temperament also had to be taken into account. It was maddeningly vague, and when all else failed, people who fell ill, or their loved ones, would pray to the saints.

Humorism would dominate Western medical prac-

Hippocrates thought behavior and temperament were influenced by the balance, or imbalance, of the four humors in the body. This early-sixteenth-century woodcut shows these human representation of humors, with their representative animals: Choleric, with lion; Sanguine, with ape; Phlegmatic, with sheep; and Melancholic, with pig.

tice for more than two thousand years, before newly published scientific discoveries in cellular anatomy, pathology, microbiology, and germ theory finally and thoroughly discredited the approach in the mid-nineteenth century. But in the mid-sixteenth century, when chocolate first made its way to Spain and then across Europe, modern medicine was still two hundred years in the future. Humorism ruled the day and influenced everything from medical prescriptions to dietary choices. There was no clear line between what was considered a medicine and what was clearly a food.

When Philip II of Spain received word of the supposed curative powers of the exotic cacao tree, he dispatched his royal physician, Francisco Hernández de Toledo, to New Spain to investigate. Hernández set sail in 1570 and stayed in Mexico for five years. Later, in 1615, he published a startlingly compr>ensive botanical encyclopedia that presented, in great detail, the plants of New Spain, including descriptions of more than three thousand species, along with the Nahuatl (Aztec) names for each one and illustrations by native artists. Not surprisingly, this record included the physician's classification of each plant as hot or cold and wet or dry.

Chocolate, Hernández advised, was cold and dry. Therefore, he concluded, drinking chocolate could be most properly used to treat fevers and other hot and wet diseases. For the same reason, he said, drinking chocolate would be most beneficial to people who lived in hot climates (who just happened to include the native Mexicans who may have invented it in the first place!). But since chocolate was cold and dry, it risked causing a state of melancholy in those who drank it, as a result of an excessive concentration of black bile. If, however, lukewarm chocolate was mixed with a few anise seeds, the result could be a more balanced temperament. Those of a cold, wet temperament, known as phlegmatic, should be given a hot and spicy chocolate drink instead.

It was complicated.

Chocolate originally had been valued as a drink that provided sustenance and energy. But as the drink spread across Europe and eventually found its way back across the Atlantic to North America, it was promoted mostly for its presumed medicinal benefits. As early as 1712, a Boston apothecary advertised chocolate for sale in his shop, and for the rest of that century chocolate was widely prescribed for the prevention and treatment of many ailments, even for the deadly smallpox virus. This was ironic indeed, considering that it was smallpox—brought by the Europeans— that had all but wiped out the Native Americans who had introduced them to chocolate in the first place.

Medicinal chocolate was being touted throughout Europe during this same period. More than twenty years after publishing his *Species Plantarum*, in which he gave the cacao tree its enduring scientific name, *Theobroma cacao*, the great Swedish taxonomist Carl Linnaeus weighed in on the medicinal benefits of the plant. In particular, he promoted the use of chocolate for treating three major classes of medical disorders that now seem wildly dissimilar: body wasting due to diseases of the lungs or muscles, hypochondria, and hemorrhoids.

////////////////

In America in the 1700s, chocolate was called a confection, but the meaning of the word then differed from the way we understand it today. Confections meant flavorings — usually sugary ones — that were mixed into medicines to disguise the bad taste. A confectioner was the person who did the mixing — often a physician or an apothecary (today known as a druggist or pharmacist). It was later that *confection* came to mean candy. By the second half of the nineteenth century, a young candy entrepreneur like Milton Hershey would call his products confections. But the line between medicine and food remained fuzzy for years. Chocolate was both a medicine given out by confectioners and a food prescribed by doctors. Both professions touted it as a kind of superfood with healing powers — much as the Mesoamericans had thought of it. But now doctors and nutritionists were giving it their professional stamp of approval, backed up by what they claimed was scientific proof. A 1905 brochure for Hershey's new chocolate company advertised his signature milk chocolate this way: *Hershey's Milk Chocolate: "More Sustaining than Meat — A Sweet to Eat!"* Another early ad that attempted to say it all called Hershey's cocoa *"A Food to Drink."*

////////////

In 1858, the German biologist, pathologist, writer, statesman, and physician Rudolf Virchow published the first of his transformative observations of cellular biology and pathology. In the years that followed, two millennia of medical dogma was overturned. The system of humors and temperaments was out, and with it went belief in the infinite therapeutic virtues attributed to chocolate. Now anyone could enjoy chocolate, regardless of individual temperament or predominant humors. The consumption of chocolate and sugar shot up dramatically, and chocolate was reborn — no longer a medicine, now a wholesome and nutritious food.

By the early twentieth century, chocolate's "healthiness" was expressed in terms of purity and nutrition — both qualities that sold well to mothers of young children. Vitamin content became another selling point; ads for chocolate quoted "leading dieticians" who claimed that chocolate, especially when combined with milk, provided an especially nourishing food. It could build strong bones and muscles, provide needed energy, and give children and adults essential vitamins and minerals. The fact that it tasted delicious was almost beside the point! Soon enough, chocolate was being touted as a kind of superfood—handy and portable, a chocolate bar could provide quick energy and strength. Power and pep! As America entered the Second World War, it was no surprise that chocolate, advertised by Nestlé in 1940 as a "Fighting Food," became literally a fighting food when special military rations of solid chocolate given to American soldiers. It wasn't the first time; one-ounce cakes of chocolate and sugar had been distributed to troops in World War I, and drinking chocolate had gone to war with American soldiers in every major American military conflict since the first one in 1776. Returning soldiers brought their fondness for chocolate with them to civilian life.

But by the late twentieth century, chocolate had become less of a power food and more of a dessert. Baked into cakes and pies, shaped into bars of chocolate, milk, and sugar that could be eaten anywhere, anytime, or wrapped up as bite-size sweets now called *chocolates*, the sacred food of the Aztecs had been transformed once again. Now it was a guilty pleasure—high in fat, sugar, and calories. It couldn't possibly be healthful, but it still tasted great.

WHY WE LOVE CHOCOLATE: THE SCIENCE OF TASTE

Of all the possible flavors on earth, why is it the taste of chocolate that more people crave than any other? Most humans are born with a preference for sweet-tasting foods, but why chocolate, specifically, more than hard candies or sweet potatoes or a juicy orange?

The physiology of taste is more complex than it may seem. It involves not just the tongue, with its built-in flavor sensors. What we perceive as taste also depends on signals from the inner lining of the cheeks and from the palate, nose, eyes, and brain. It's a total sensory experience.

Smell accounts for about 90 percent of how we perceive taste. Aromas, or odors, in foods and other substances are caused by volatile chemicals — compounds that evaporate, transporting the essence of their scent to the nose, specifically to special sensory tissue in the back of the nasal cavity. Chocolate contains more than six hundred volatile chemicals, which together produce the classic chocolate aroma that is hard to describe but is instantly recognizable. You can almost taste a piece of chocolate fudge or a brownie before you put it into your mouth!

For those who love chocolate, the next step —

assuming that chocolate *does* meet mouth — follows quickly. The human mouth is a highly sensitive chemical detector, able to distinguish sweet, sour, salty, bitter, and umami (a savory flavor officially made the fifth taste in 1985) in as little as .0015 seconds. In fact, the sense of taste is faster than either touch or vision — probably because accuracy in the taste function can be a matter of life and death. Ten thousand taste buds — clusters of specialized cells that are spread over the tongue, palate, and inner cheek — act as an early warning signal to ensure that a food is safe, not toxic. Sweet equals safe, thinks the brain, and bitter, in many cases, is construed to mean not safe!

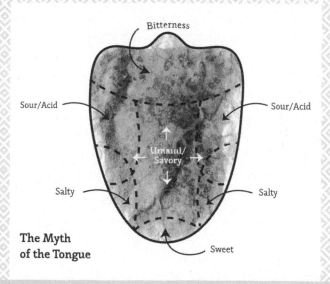

Bitterness

Sour/Acid

Sour/Acid

Umami/
Savory

Salty

Salty

The Myth
of the Tongue

Sweet

This tongue mapping has been discredited by more recent science, but was once believed to be true. Many people still believe it is!

Texture plays an important part in flavor too. Recently, it's been proposed that humans may have special taste receptors for fat. Since fat provided our ancestors with needed energy and essential fatty acids, it shares top billing with sweetness on most people's favorites list, though saltiness is a close third. We naturally crave the creamy texture of fat, and cocoa butter, the natural fat that is contained in chocolate, adds greatly to the sensory pleasure we get from eating it. Chocolate in the hand is hard and brittle, but because cocoa butter's melting point is just below the human body temperature, chocolate in the mouth transforms almost instantly to smooth, velvety deliciousness.

Cultural differences influence taste as well; relatively little chocolate is consumed in China, for example, though this could change with rising global trade. There's also evidence that psychology contributes a lot to how we experience tastes. Researchers in Spain and the United Kingdom have reported experimental evidence showing that the color of the cup affects how much a person may enjoy the taste of a nice, steaming cup of hot chocolate. It turns out that chocolate seems to taste better in an orange or cream-colored cup than in a white or red one. These findings were published in 2012 in the *Journal of Sensory Studies*. Another study published that year in the journal *Psychological Science* found that, with chocolate as with life, most people tend to perceive the last chocolate they ate to be the one that tastes best, regardless of flavor (mild, dark, caramel, or almond). It seems that endings are bittersweet.

Perhaps because it is so very delicious, chocolate has been looked upon, in some quarters, with moral disapproval. Whether for moral reasons or aesthetic ones—waistlines can be a concern—chocolate is complicated by questions of good and evil, and for many, it's forbidden fruit. Maybe it's a holdover from the chocolate-as-medicine days; we talk of being "addicted" to it, of being a "chocoholic." Restaurant menus describe a dense slice of chocolate cake as "sinfully" or "wickedly" rich. Decadent. We crave "devil's food cake," or even what marketers call Death by Chocolate. Bring it on.

This is not a new phenomenon. Chocolate consumption was a culturally acceptable substitute for alcohol among elite Aztecs, but they were still deeply conflicted about it. The drink they borrowed from the Maya, their cultured neighbors in the tropical lowlands, was seen as exotic and luxurious. Drinking it went against the image that the Aztecs held of themselves as an austere people who had clawed their way up from extreme poverty and hardship to the height of affluence, power, and abundance in less than two hundred years. So even though a deeply puritanical streak in Aztec culture made chocolate seem somehow more acceptable than alcohol, the spicy drink of the Maya came with its own burden of discomfort.

Morality was a primary motivator for the Quakers of nineteenth-century England, too. They viewed chocolate as a much more wholesome and "good" drink than popular alcoholic beverages of the day, and promoted it to persuade the poor, especially, to abstain from drinking spirits. A hundred years later the whole notion of "good" chocolate would be turned on its head again. It's hard not to see how history keeps repeating itself.

In America, a country founded in part by Puritans, an ingrained "truth" is that to deny ourselves the things we crave is a virtue. If so, then it would be very virtuous to deprive oneself of chocolate, the most highly craved food of all. And so it came to be. In the latter part of the twentieth century, a long list of the evils of chocolate, starting with its high fat and sugar content, began to demonize the food of the gods. It was no longer a cure-all. On the contrary, chocolate caused acne. It was the source of migraine headaches, allergies, hyperactivity, and dental cavities. And if it was an aid to romance, as some claimed, was that a good thing?

By the 1980s, though, scientists had begun to treat

seriously the question of whether chocolate consumption is actually bad for human health. The research showed that most of the terrible things chocolate was widely believed to cause were not associated with eating it after all. Multiple studies concluded that chocolate has no causal relationship to acne, the guilt and fear factor that had long been at the top of the list. Tooth decay was also quickly crossed off; chocolate contains a tannin that blocks the production of an enzyme that causes dental plaque (the first step in tooth decay). Moreover, the cocoa butter that is naturally found in chocolate acts to coat the teeth, thus countering the cavity-causing potential of chocolate candy's high sugar content. There was no scientific evidence of allergic reactions to chocolate, and no evidence that eating it caused migraine headaches. No link was found between chocolate and hyperactivity disorders, either in children or adults.

It's true that chocolate is calorie-dense and high in sugar and fat, but that can be said of many foods that are known to be good for us, at least in moderation. Like olive oil and nuts, scientists have found, chocolate can be a healthful food, though a little of it goes a long way.

Chocolate is highly complex. More than six hundred chemical compounds, so far, have been identified within the seed of the cacao tree. So, having dismissed most of the myths of chocolate's evils, scientists at the turn of the twenty-first century set about to determine whether chocolate might be beneficial to human health.

Cocoa beans contain approximately 50 percent fat, and a fatty diet is associated with a host of medical problems, including obesity, high cholesterol, diabetes, and some cancers. But scientists now understand that the *type* of fat in a food is at least as important as the amount of fat. The fat in chocolate comprises two different saturated fatty acids (stearic and palmitic) and one unsaturated fat (oleic acid). It turns out that the fats in cocoa butter and in dark chocolate do not elevate blood cholesterol. Many studies have shown that regular consumption of small amounts of dark chocolate may actually *lower* the level of LDL, or "bad" cholesterol, and raise HDL, the "good" cholesterol! And when this occurs, other important health benefits follow, such as improved blood flow and a reduced risk of stroke and heart disease.

As to sugar, the average dark chocolate bar contains about 25 grams. Many health professionals have become increasingly concerned about negative health consequences of the higher sugar content in our modern diet. But 25 grams of sugar is considerably less than the amount in a 12-ounce can of soda (39 grams) or in a cup of fruity yogurt with sugar added (27 grams), and only slightly more than the amount in a single large apple (23 grams). It's also been shown that on average, chocolate products account for no more than 1 percent of the calories we take in every day. While it's true that obesity is a serious problem, chocolate is not the culprit in the vast majority of cases.

The key is this: All chocolate is not created equal. The greater the percentage of cocoa solids, the smaller the amount of sugar, and the greater the health benefit. Many makers of dark chocolate have begun listing the percentage of cocoa in their bars and candies. Unsweetened cocoa, for drinking and for baking, is loaded with cocoa solids, too.

///////////////

So it seems that chocolate isn't really bad for us, but can it possibly be good in even more ways? What about those six-hundred-plus chemical compounds? Cocoa beans contain polyphenols (similar to the ones that are found in red wine), which have antioxidant properties. These compounds are called flavonoids, and one of them, epicatechin, seems especially useful for reducing blood pressure and stimulating blood flow to the brain, hands, and legs. Epicatechin can also reduce the blood's ability to clot; it functions in much the same way that a daily baby aspirin does, but it's in a much tastier way. This, too, reduces the risk of stroke and heart attack. Now scientists suspect that antioxidants may also play a role in helping to prevent or delay dementia, arthritis, asthma, and many cancers. Other studies suggest that cocoa extract can be a safe, effective remedy for potentially life-threatening diarrhea in children.

Dark chocolate is one of the top antioxidant foods, equal to or greater than so-called superfoods such as blueberries, cranberries, and red beans in its antioxidant properties.

Scientists are also working to uncover the reasons that chocolate seems to make us feel good when we eat it. A number of its naturally occurring chemical compounds are known to have psychological effects; the most important of these compounds are caffeine, theobromine, serotonin, phenylethylamine, and anandamide.

Nearly everyone is familiar with the effects of caffeine. It improves alertness, energy, and focus. It can also be addictive if consumed in large quantities over

Chocolate pills in a blister pack: less fun than a panful of fudge brownies?

a period of time, and it can cause sleeplessness and heart palpitations. But chocolate contains only a tiny amount of caffeine, much less than is found in coffee, tea, or colas. Theobromine is a stimulant that in some ways is similar to caffeine, but unlike caffeine it is not found in many other foods. There's more of it in chocolate than in tea, which contains only trace amounts, but theobromine is a much milder stimulant than caffeine. It may have about the same stimulating effect as drinking a can of cola, but hardly anyone would think of eating a piece of chocolate to stay awake, and for good reason.

Serotonin, phenylethylamine, and anandamide are associated with mood changes and other psychological effects. Seratonin is a naturally occurring brain chemical that contributes to feelings of well-being; people who suffer from depression, and women who experience symptoms of PMS, often have decreased seratonin levels. Eating chocolate or drinking cocoa increases the level of this chemical in the brain, which may help explain why many people find they feel happier after consuming cocoa-rich foods.

Phenylethylamine, another naturally occurring brain chemical, is present in chocolate at higher levels than caffeine, and it's a powerful molecule that is related to amphetamines. It triggers the release of other chemicals in the brain—chemicals that generate intensely good feelings. People who are falling in love have been shown to have increased levels of phenylethylamine in their brain. But eating foods with fat and sugar raises phenylethylamine levels, too, and the amount of this chemical in chocolate is a lot lower than the amount that is found in salami and cheddar cheese. So by itself, this chemical probably can't explain the uniquely feel-good powers of chocolate. It may be that no one chemical in chocolate, but rather its unique combination of chemical compounds, produces the happy feeling that is so widely associated with eating it.

Anandamide may explain a lot as well. No one knew this molecule existed until the early 1990s, when researchers who were looking into the effects of marijuana found another naturally occurring "pleasure" chemical, completely unrelated to phenylethylamine, in the human brain. Daniel Piomelli, a researcher at the Neurosciences Institute in San Diego, California, named the chemical anandamide, which means "bliss" in Sanskrit. It turns out that anandamide has a chemical shape that is nearly identical to the shape of the psychoactive chemical that resides in marijuana.

The human brain has built-in receptors for a molecule of this shape, which is why marijuana often produces pleasurable feelings in those who use it.

Sure enough, when Piomelli looked at chocolate, he found that it contains anandamide. This, he thought, might help to explain the chocolate cravings that people have described ever since the days of New Spain. So far, chocolate and marijuana are the only known sources of these molecular twins, but the level of anandamide is far lower in chocolate than the level of the psychoactive chemical in marijuana. A person would have to eat at least twenty-five pounds of chocolate to get any kind of "high" from it, but two other compounds that have been discovered in chocolate act to increase the activity of anandamide in the brain. These enzymes may help to prolong a mellow but mild sense of well-being after eating chocolate. Scientists are studying chocolate's anandamide effect in the hope that the research may lead to the development of better, safer antidepressant drugs.

//////////////

The more we learn about the complex chemical properties and healing abilities of cacao, the more distant it can seem from the simple, spindly rainforest tree that produces it. But remember: Chocolate begins with the seed of that tree, and the seed begins with the pod, and the pod grows only with the help of an insect so small you can barely see it. And the fruit of that tree was first a food and still is. So it is with chocolate.

In fact, a nutritional analysis of dark chocolate reveals that it looks a lot like . . . food. A 1.5-ounce bar contains nearly 2 grams of protein, 2.6 grams of fiber, 210 calories, 28 grams of carbohydrates, 13 grams of fat, and many essential minerals, including magnesium, calcium, iron, zinc, copper, potassium, and manganese. It also provides vitamins A, B_1, B_2, B_3, C, E, and pantothenic acid.

So is it candy, food, or medicine?

The answer is, all three! And with so much going for chocolate, it's hard to find a reason not to indulge a little. Now scientists are developing better ways to identify and preserve the very best of the world's living cacao and to grow it more sustainably. With each advance in the science of chocolate, and in the reform of exploitative labor practices in the cacao industry, indulging can feel more and more guilt-free.

At the same time, scientists are exploring the intricacies of chocolate genetics, and are helping to piece together the long history of the cacao tree, as well as its future.

BUT NOT FOR DOGS!

Though chocolate can be considered a health food for humans, it's poisonous to dogs, cats, horses, and some other animals. The problem is the theobromine that chocolate contains and, to a lesser extent, the caffeine. Eating a lot of fat and sugar is also not good for dogs, and in large quantities these substances can make them very ill. Both theobromine and caffeine can be toxic to humans, but the amount needed to cause problems is much greater, because humans tend to be larger than most dogs and cats, and more important, we are able to metabolize the two alkaloids much more quickly and efficiently. Even a small amount of chocolate can be deadly for cats, but since they have no taste receptors for sweetness, they're unlikely to sample a chocolate bar they find on the kitchen counter. It's different with dogs. Though eating a small amount of chocolate is rarely fatal to the family dog, it can be fatal if the dog is small, or if the amount and type of chocolate that the dog consumes — the higher the cocoa percentage, the greater the risk — is more than he or she can safely digest. Symptoms of theobromine poisoning in dogs can include intestinal distress, increased urination, racing heartbeat, extreme anxiousness, seizures, coma, and, in the worst-case scenario, death. Keeping all chocolate products out of reach of dogs is always a good idea.

RECIPE

Mexican Hot Chocolate

From "A Chocolate Guide: A User's Manual," Carol Taylor, *Mother Earth News*, November/December 1988.

2 ounces unsweetened chocolate, grated

¼ cup boiling water

2 cups milk, warmed

1 cup heavy cream, warmed

3 tablespoons sugar

1 teaspoon cinnamon

Pinch of cloves

Pinch of salt

1 egg

1 teaspoon vanilla extract

❖ *Melt chocolate in a medium double boiler over hot water. Add boiling water and mix well. Stir in milk and cream, then the sugar, spices, and salt. Whisk mixture over medium low heat until it comes to a boil, reduce heat to simmer, and cook for 5 minutes, whisking continuously.*

❖ *In a separate bowl, beat egg with vanilla until frothy. Add a little of the hot chocolate (reheat it if necessary) to the egg, stir well, then add egg to the remaining chocolate. Beat with electric hand mixer or rotary beater for 3 minutes over low heat. Pour into coffee cups and serve immediately. Serves 4.*

In Search of Wild Chocolate:
New Science Meets Ancient Trees

After a detailed study of the centers where the forms of cultivated plants were created, a botanist acquires the right to dispute the conclusions drawn by historians and archaeologists.

—Nikolai Vavilov

Lyndel Meinhardt brushed away the sweat that was dripping down his brow from beneath the baseball cap he wore to ward off mosquitoes and the hot tropical sun. He waited, taking time to catch his breath while the machete-wielding guide hacked through thick underbrush in the Peruvian rainforest and cleared a path to the first stop of the day's trek. It was July 2008, and Lyndel was leading an international team of scientists on an eight-day expedition through the Amazon rainforest of Peru. The object of the search: discovering a few wild cacao trees that Lyndel hoped would have pods containing both fine-flavor beans and natural resistance to the deadly diseases — witches' broom, frosty pod, and black pod — that commonly infect *Theobroma cacao*.

It's this destructive trio, as much as anything, that has Lyndel and other plant scientists worried. Very worried. At least 30 to 40 percent of the world's cacao crop is lost every year to these diseases, and to insect pests like mirids and cocoa pod borers. After witches' broom all but destroyed the cacao industry in Ecuador and Trinidad earlier in the twentieth century, it invaded Brazil in the late 1980s, cutting that country's crop in half by the year 2010. If the dreaded fungi, already firmly established in South and Central America, continue to spread, they could jump the Atlantic and infect trees in West Africa, currently the largest cacao-producing region in the world. Black pod — not a true fungus but a water-loving mold — is already entrenched there. With worldwide demand for chocolate continuing to rise, the race is on to identify and cultivate naturally disease-resistant strains of cacao, and to find new ways of protecting cacao trees with the use of beneficial fungi and better management practices. Preserving and even improving the dwindling supply of really special cocoa beans — the coveted, unique fine-flavor beans that are the fastest-growing segment of the market — is another mandate. Failure is not an option; it would mean that the world's chocolate supply could be seriously endangered within a few years.

FINE FLAVOR

The world cocoa market distinguishes between two broad categories of cacao beans: fine flavor and bulk beans. As a generalization, fine flavor cacao beans are produced from Criollo or Trinitario varieties, while bulk cacao beans come from Forastero trees. But there are important exceptions. Nacional (see page 200) trees in Ecuador, considered to be the Forastero type, produce fine-flavor cocoa. On the other hand, although Cameroon cacao beans are produced by Trinitario trees, they are classified as bulk beans, and the cocoa powder made from them has a distinct and sought-after red color. It's no wonder that chocolate connoisseurs spend years sorting it all out.

Wild cacao trees often cluster near rainforest rivers. Lyndel's team was searching near several branches of the Marañón, Peru's longest river and a major source for the Amazon. The Marañón River begins north of Lima and flows north a thousand miles before forming the headwaters of the Amazon as it churns northeast toward the Atlantic Ocean. Along the way it carves

A typical Peruvian village on the banks of the Pastaza River, a large tributary of the Marañón River in the northwestern Amazon basin. Two wild cacao populations were sampled upstream from here.

out many isolated, hard-to-access canyons, each with its own microclimate and its own animal and plant populations. The cacao trees that grow wild, hidden away in these river canyons, have likely lived there for centuries and were probably planted by ancient tribes, by acts of nature, or both.

July is the dry season in Peru, or as dry as it ever gets in a rainforest, which doesn't mean that the scientists never got wet. For the most part the weather was cooperating. The team comprised scientists from two divisions at the U.S. Department of Agriculture's Agricultural Research Service in Beltsville, Maryland: the Sustainable Perennial Crops Laboratory and the Systematic Mycology and Microbiology Laboratory. Mycology is the study of fungi, and the top mycologist on this expedition was veteran Gary Samuels. The geneticist Dapeng Zhang was also on board, along with the plant pathologist Enrique Arévalo, one of the cacao specialists from Peru's Instituto de Cultivos Tropicales (ICT) in Tarapoto.

The purpose of the expedition was at once broad and focused—to collect as many wild cacao tree samples as possible, along with samples of the fungi that cause pod-destroying diseases and of beneficial fungi that might be the natural enemies of the destructive types. Living tree samples the team collected would, by international agreement, stay in Peru, at the ICT facilities in Tarapoto, but the DNA of leaves, bark, and fungal spores would be available to the USDA/ARS for genetic analysis.

Lyndel was well suited to this mission, but he'd arrived at this junction in his career by an unconventional route. The research leader at the USDA/ARS, he's a Missouri farm boy turned tropical plant expert. He has extensive knowledge of fungal and bacterial diseases of the cacao tree. The broad focus of his research, and of the team he leads, is sustainable perennial crops—with an emphasis on "sustainable."

It's not just about chocolate, though a world without it is obviously unthinkable! With climate change models predicting more and more extreme weather in this century, Lyndel believes still-undiscovered varieties of plants may hold the genetic keys to drought- and disease-resistant crops that could help ensure the world food supply. Corn, for example, has only a few wild relatives left in nature. What scientists can learn from the DNA of wild cacao species waiting to be discovered—if they can be found before they're lost forever—could help achieve the larger goal of protecting the crops that feed the world.

Predictably, the expedition was challenging. Days were hot and humid in the rainforest, and the rough terrain made hiking difficult. But Lyndel was accustomed to difficult conditions. Growing up on the family farm, and helping to grow grain and raise cattle and hogs, he'd worked long hours from an early age, squeezing time for school in between morning and evening chores. After graduating from high school, he'd farmed full-time with his father and brother for several years, growing corn and soybeans on nine hundred acres of land and taking two thousand hogs to market each year. At age twenty-one he decided to leave the farm, but by then, working with plants and animals had become part of his identity. Especially plants.

He wanted to learn everything he could about plants and realized he could combine what he already knew with a newfound passion for science. He studied plant pathology in graduate school and took postdoctoral training in hot, humid Florida, where he studied fungal plant disease interactions. Then he began an eighteen-month visiting scientist gig in Brazil that turned into a ten-year stay. It was during those years in Brazil that he began working out the genomes of fungi that were attacking local cacao trees—research that led directly to his position with the USDA/ARS. So this expedition to the cacao-growing region of Peru felt, in a way, like coming home.

Oddly enough, Lyndel found that the steamy rainforest reminded him of a mature, late-summer cornfield back in Missouri. It was different, of course. In the cornfields, you could always see the wide-open sky, and walking between towering rows of cornstalks was easy, if a bit claustrophobic. Here in the rainforest, canopy trees that reached for the clouds—towering close to a hundred feet above the forest floor—all but blocked out the sky. Wild jungle understory trees, growing in every direction along with the thick underbrush, snatched at sleeves and hats. Hidden roots could send you sprawling.

But above all, it was the ants that let him know he wasn't in Missouri. They were ferocious. You had to be extremely careful where you stopped while walking in the rainforest; if you hesitated close to an anthill, you'd be attacked. The ants would sting until your feet and legs, and whatever other body parts they could reach, were on fire.

///////////////

There's trouble in the cacao woods nowadays, and it's not the ants. Destructive fungi and insects attack susceptible cacao trees. Climate change has begun a domino-like process of extinction, species by species, whose endgame no one can fully envision. The vast tropical rainforest itself is shrinking. Bit by bit, old forest trees are removed for their wood, and jungle is transformed into pastureland and fields for planting soybeans and other agricultural crops. In sum, human activity threatens remaining wild cacao in its native habitat, and even more worrisome, the genetic variability of cacao's germplasm is at severe risk.

Cacao trees have what Lyndel and other plant scientists call a "recalcitrant seed," which means that it loses viability very fast, unlike the seeds of many other crops, and thus cannot be preserved in cold storage. So the only way to maintain samples of cacao types is as living trees. As a result, the world's entire library of known cacao species is currently maintained in collections located in Trinidad and Costa Rica, where the climate is suitable for them.

Back in Beltsville, Maryland, a densely populated suburb of Washington, D.C. (named not for the nearby Washington Beltway, Interstate 495, but rather for the Belt family, who established a small railroad station there in the 1830s), Lyndel keeps one room-size, healthy-looking cacao tree, like an overgrown houseplant, in a pot on the floor of his cramped office on the USDA/ARS campus. A short walk from this building, rows of test trees at various stages of growth thrive in experimental greenhouses where conditions of the rainforest can be roughly simulated. But these trees are like strangers in a strange land this far north of the equator.

When he began leading the ARS project, looking at genetic diversity of the world's cacao, Lyndel quickly learned that there *isn't* much genetic diversity to be found in the living cacao database. Or rather, there isn't nearly enough diversity collected, properly identified, and available to scientists, as well as to chocolate growers and makers. One major problem is that many of the samples growing in international collections had somehow been mislabeled (a mistake that has been determined by now readily available genetic sequencing), but it also turns out that most of the plants in the collections derive from a relatively small number of wild tree samples that were collected by plant hunters more than seventy years ago.

SCIENTIST SLEUTHS, TRACKING CACAO THROUGH TIME

Scientists have been searching for the ideal cacao tree for a very long time. Following a long line of intrepid plant explorers of the eighteenth and nineteenth centuries who traveled the world, facing down tropical diseases, extreme climate and terrain, dangerous wild animals, and even life-threatening vegetation, early plant hunters were like the Indiana Joneses of the botanical world. The plants they discovered and brought back to their countries of origin gave rise to major advances in science, medicine, and agriculture that changed the world.

One such man was Nikolai Vavilov, a prominent Russian botanist, geneticist, and plant hunter who devoted his life to the study and improvement of wheat, corn, and other vital grain crops in order to help solve the problem of world hunger. From 1916 to 1940, Vavilov

Nikolai Vavilov.

traveled throughout the Middle East, the Mediterra-
nean, Africa, Asia, Central America, South America,
and the Soviet Union, and compiled an extensive
survey of the agricultural plants he found in the field.
His mission was to find wild relatives and ancestors
of cultivated plants, and over the course of his career
as director of Russia's Institute of Plant Industry, he
amassed a priceless collection of some two hundred
thousand specimens.

As he traveled the world, observing and collecting crop plants, Vavilov was struck by a very big idea: the place where there was the greatest diversity of a particular plant species, he theorized, must also be the place in which that species had originated. By 1926, he was sure of it. He mapped out the regions he called "centers of diversity" and put his idea out to the scientific community. It's an idea that has held up, along with his maps, for more than eighty years and has come to be regarded as a basic principle by the generations of biologists who have followed him.

Vavilov was convinced that the cacao tree had originated in Mexico, where it grew in abundance. Even though his general theory of diversity centers would be proven correct, this crucial detail turned out to be wrong. More important, Vavilov's big idea about where species originate, and his refusal to compromise or recant it, wound up costing him his life. It had aroused deep resentment in Stalin's favorite agronomist, a science doubter named Trofim Lysenko, who had Vavilov arrested in 1940 on trumped-up charges of spying and vaguely specified agricultural crimes. Three years later Vavilov died in prison from malnutrition, a sad fate for a visionary scientist who had hoped, more than anything, to increase the world's food supply.

It fell to other plant explorers to provide evidence that would reveal the cacao tree's true birthplace. In the late 1930s and early 1940s, F. J. Pound of Trinidad's Imperial College (now part of the University of the West Indies) searched the Upper Amazon for ca-

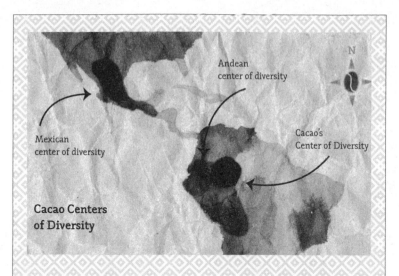

Andean
center of diversity

Mexican
center of diversity

Cacao's
Center of Diversity

N

**Cacao Centers
of Diversity**

cao trees that were resistant to witches' broom, which had decimated pods in Trinidad and Ecuador. Pound, who is acknowledged as the pioneer of the genetic improvement of cacao, had previously observed trees that showed apparent resistance to the fungus that was growing in Ecuador. During Pound's further travels, he was able to identify at least one resistant variety, but that tree had the disadvantage of growing smaller pods with fewer seeds. Perhaps even more important than this discovery in the search for cacao's origins was another observation that Pound made. Overall, he was amazed by the enormous diversity of cacao he found growing in this region.

It would be the English botanist E. E. Cheesman who in 1944 combined Vavilov's and Pound's observations, and deduced that the cocoa tree had originated not in Mexico, as Vavilov had thought, but rather in the Upper

Amazon region of South America, Vavilov's "Andean Center of Diversity." This conclusion has since been confirmed many times over by modern plant scientists.

Thanks to the discoveries of Vavilov, Pound, and Cheesman, today's cocoa researchers know where to look for new and undiscovered chocolate strains: the area where Peru, Ecuador, and Colombia hug the Pacific — touching Brazil on its northwestern border — and where numerous tributaries of the great Amazon River etch trails through deeply eroded, ancient ground on their way to the sea.

///////////////

Before they arrived in the summer of 2008, the scientists on Lyndel's team had no idea whether they'd be able to find any wild cacao trees growing in the rainforest. But on the very first day of the expedition, they got their answer to that question: a resounding yes. There were so many trees that the challenge would be collecting even a fraction of the different varieties during the time they had.

On the day before they set out on their search, the team pitched tents in a village near their first collecting site. The next morning, they woke to rooster calls. That first workday, and the ones that followed it, started before dawn. It was chilly before daybreak,

Gary Samuels (left) and Lyndel Meinhardt (center), researchers with the USDA's Agricultural Research Service, and the plant pathologist Enrique Arévalo, of the Instituto de Cultivos Tropicales in Peru, examine cacao leaves that have been infected with witches' broom.

and the tents were dripping with dew. Lyndel and the others crawled out of their sleeping bags, packed their equipment, and loaded it into waiting boats. Everything, every surface, was as wet with dew as the tents. Still groggy, the scientists clambered into the boats, and the guides pushed off onto the river. Most of the researchers tried to find comfortable positions on the damp boats and drift back to sleep until they had to go to work.

The boats stopped at villages along the route. On

some days the men enjoyed a simple prearranged breakfast, purchased from a local family. But more often the group headed straight into the forest to begin the day's collecting. One advance team member left ahead of the others with a local guide who knew the way to the nearby wild cacao trees, and the two men cut their way through the forest to the first tree of the day, to which they attached a numbered aluminum tag. The rest of the team followed close behind, and when they reached the tree, they got down to work.

One person recorded the pertinent details—GPS location, tree height, trunk diameter, and so on. Another collected soil samples, while someone else carefully removed a branch so that leaf samples and stems could be collected. Working together, two other people cut away a section of the tree's bark, scraping with a sharp blade in search of possible fungi underneath. Lyndel's job was to take cuttings from each tree, dip them into a nutrient solution, and carefully bag them for the trip back to Tarapoto.

The scientists tried to collect material from about ten to fifteen trees at each location; then they climbed into the boats and moved two or three miles upriver to the next destination. Working at three or four sites took most of the day, and as the day grew later, the air grew hotter and downright steamy. Lyndel found himself looking forward to each short boat ride between collecting sites; the forward movement stirred up a small breeze on the water that helped revive him. In between stops, the scientists snacked on canned tuna and saltines, and guzzled water to stay hydrated.

As demanding as these days in the rainforest could be, they were also exhilarating. A group of botanists walking through the Peruvian Amazon, one of the most biologically diverse regions on earth, is a bit like kids turned loose in a candy store. For the Americans, who were unaccustomed to the sights and sounds of a rainforest, it was a feast for the senses.

At the end of each day's work, the scientists climbed back into their boats and traveled to the next village, where they set up camp all over again. Then they headed back down to the river to wash off the day's sweat and grime, and to scrub their clothes. By that time, night would be approaching. The Peruvians would have hired a family from the village to cook dinner for the scientists. Sometimes it was boiled salted fish and plantains, sometimes rice and chicken or another entrée, but the plant collectors were hungry by the time they joined their hosts for dinner, and it all tasted delicious.

After the meal, the scientists often showed an educational movie to the villagers, using a generator to power lights and a projector. The local people had little access to electricity, let alone films, and they were fascinated. By the time the scientists crawled into their tents for the night, it was still hot and steamy, but they were too tired to care. Not too tired, though, to zip up their tents and make sure they had done everything they could to keep mosquitoes out. Next to the ants, the mosquitoes and the chiggers were the worst.

The days went by fast, and by the end of the two wefis, the team had explored seven river systems and had sampled 190 wild cacao trees. Of these, 128 would be successfully reestablished in the living germplasm bank in Tarapoto. But that was just part of what the team accomplished. Lyndel had also recorded evidence of witches' broom disease everywhere they searched. He'd graded the severity of disease in each tree, based on a percentage of symptoms in the flower cushions, new stem growth, and fruits.

Coming from a cacao pathologist, Lyndel's analysis was stunning: here, protecting these wild Peruvian cacao populations, was a high level of resistance to witches' broom disease. DNA samples of trees and fungi would be analyzed in the coming months to determine which trees were the best, most flavorful, and most disease resistant.

The USDA/ARS mycologist Gary Samuels brought

Using a sterile technique, Gary Samuels extracts a sample of living plant tissue from a wild cacao tree on the banks of the Marañón River. Fungi in the sample could prove useful as a biological control agent for important cacao pathogens.

back samples of what might be called "friendly fungi"—endophytic fungi that occur in the disease-free tissues of all plants. Those he'd collected from the leaves and trunks of wild Peruvian cacao trees might reveal, under microscopic analysis, how they protect their tree hosts. Was it by stimulating the tree's immune system or some other means? As with the cacao trees themselves, several previously unknown fungi species had been collected and identified. In time, these fungi may provide new biocontrol methods for making cacao trees healthier and more productive.

In 2009, members of the team returned to explore five more river systems. They collected and reestablished 152 trees, with the result that three new populations of wild cacao, previously unknown to science, have now been identified for further testing. The new strains may possess unique, new flavor traits and may provide vital sources of disease resistance.

The benefits of these collecting trips will soon find their way out of the labs at Beltsville and Tarapoto and into the real world of chocolate. When scientists have identified desirable traits from the collections in Peru, cacao plant breeders will be able to transplant these traits from wild cacao trees into trees that can be cultivated on cacao farms.

A lot of cacao trees remain to be explored in the Amazon rainforest. It will take time, because these trees need years to grow and mature before they produce cacao beans. But by learning the genomes of the trees and their fungi, and knowing how to use this information, science could open up a whole new age of chocolate. Once the wild trees produce beans, their individual flavor profiles can be evaluated; propagating more of the trees that produce the finest flavors would then be possible.

Scientific research, of course, requires both expertise and funding. Expertise is available in abundance, but funding can often be a challenge, and when it is, research lags behind. So it was a fortunate collaboration between the chocolate industry and government that recently culminated in the sequencing of the cacao genome. Geneticists who accomplished that feat are now working hard to identify old and new varieties. Every bit of new information that is placed in the genetic data bank increases the chances of fighting back against problems that threaten the world's supply of chocolate. If scientists can identify particular gene variants that are linked to traits like desirable taste, disease resistance, and higher crop yield in wild trees, they'll be able to cultivate new crops of these improved versions of the ancient tree. But first they have to find the originals.

Enter the Great Cacao Genome Project Race.

////////////////////

In 2003, the Human Genome Project was completed. Through an international collaboration that lasted more than a decade, the entire genetic sequence of the human body was mapped. Scientists predicted that major advances in human medicine would follow, and some advances have begun to emerge. The genomes of more than 180 organisms have been sequenced since 1995, and in 2008 scientists announced that work was under way to sequence the genome of the cacao tree. The cacao genome (420 million base pairs) turned out to be far smaller than the human genome (3 billion base pairs); that was a lucky break, because sequencing the cacao genome was a race in more ways than one. First, it was seen as a race against time, as analysts were warning that world demand for chocolate could outstrip supply by a million tons as early as the year 2020. Demand is soaring, as Asian populations who had never consumed much chocolate but are now eager to have it. On the supply side, climate change, deforestation, poverty that forces many small farmers to sell their land, global pressure to eliminate child labor, and cacao's susceptibility to disease all negatively affect the ability of growers to keep up with rising demand.

But the project to sequence the cacao genome also turned into a race between two competing scientific teams, each affiliated with one of the two b›emoths of Big Chocolate — Mars and Hershey. These companies have a long history of intense and sometimes bitter competition, so maybe it was predictable that early plans to work cooperatively on sequencing the genome of the plant on which both companies depend would go awry. When they did, the two research groups proceeded independently. On the Mars A-team of scientists: the Agricultural Research Service of the U.S. Department of Agriculture, Indiana University, and the giant tech company IBM. On the Hershey team: equally top-notch scientists from Pennsylvania State University, with support from the French government and other research institutions.

The two teams shared a common objective: the use of molecular biology to improve yields and create cacao varieties that are more resistant to disease but that still taste great and offer the most beneficial flavonoids. Each team selected a different variety of cacao tree to analyze. Mars, whose scientists got off to a head start, chose the world's most commonly cultivated type, the green-podded Costa Rican Matina, a variety of Amelonado, which is a type of Forastero cacao. This is the bean most commonly found in the so-called bulk chocolate that major candy companies use in their products worldwide.

Hershey and Penn State chose, instead, the ancient

Criollo variety—one of the rarest today in its original form, prized for its fine flavor since the Maya first cultivated it centuries ago, but highly susceptible to disease.

In the end, it was a near tie, and for chocolate lovers, it was all good. The Mars consortium was first to publish its map of the genome in the fall of 2010; the Hershey group soon followed with its results. Scientists from both groups said that having *two* cacao genomes sequenced, from different varieties, would benefit cacao farmers, candy companies, and chocolate lovers everywhere. Mark Guiltinan, a professor of plant molecular biology at Penn State and a key member of the Hershey team, said, "Understanding the chocolate genome will have so many benefits. Perennial tree crops like cacao are good for the soil. They protect the water shed and provide habitat for insects, birds, and other animals." Ultimately, Guiltinan is most interested in improving cacao varieties for the people who grow them. He sees cacao as a means to economic, environmental, and social improvement. About 45 million people worldwide depend on cacao for their livelihood; using proven scientific methods to increase the productivity of their small-acreage groves will help lift many out of poverty.

Juan Carlos Motamayor, cacao geneticist and head of the Mars team, is equally positive about the prospects for using the new science to help small cacao growers.

"Our strategy is to increase land efficiency," he said. "We try to promote growing cocoa in less space." Doing so would help farmers to diversify their crops and boost incomes, said Dr. Motamayor. With an estimated two hundred thousand small-scale family cacao farms in West and Central Africa, many barely getting by, increasing land efficiency could make the difference between failure and success more robust harvests and greater prosperity for growers.

Now scientists understand that instead of just three basic types of cacao — Criollo, Forastero, and Trinitario — there are at least ten. That's how many different "genetic clusters" Motamayor has identified so far, from samples taken in various geographic locations. There may be more. Genetic analysis is allowing plant scientists to understand better how genetics and place of origin affect how hardy a cacao tree will be, what gives its beans their unique flavor, and how best to improve the productivity of cacao plantings on which families — and chocolate lovers everywhere — depend.

RECIPE

Ecuadorian Hot Chocolate

2 cups milk
1 ounce bittersweet chocolate
4 tablespoons cocoa powder
4 tablespoons brown sugar
1 dash salt
2 eggs
2 ounces cream cheese
1 dash cinnamon

❖ Heat the milk in a saucepan, being careful not to let it boil.

❖ Add chocolate, cocoa powder, salt, and brown sugar. Mix, stirring constantly.

❖ Pour half the mixture into a blender, add eggs and cream cheese, blend on high till foamy.

❖ Return to saucepan, stir to mix, serve immediately. Garnish with a sprinkle of cinnamon.

The Mother Tree and the Accidental Chocolate Makers

This history begins with a tree, a spindly understory tree, content to grow in the shade of buttress-rooted giants.

—Michael D. Coe and Sophie D. Coe,
The True History of Chocolate, 2013

In a hidden canyon carved through ancient Andean rock by time and the mighty Marañón River, the mother tree tilts her leaves languidly into the humid afternoon air.

She's an unassuming tree — you might even call her scrawny. She has an almost fragile-looking trunk and scraggly, haphazard branches, all splotched with patches of lichen and moss. But her shiny green and tender reddish leaves glow with health; ripening pods in shades of yellow, green, and deep red add more splashes of color. The tree grows in a cluster with others of her kind, more than halfway up a mountain at 3,500 feet above sea level, overlooking an emerald-carpeted expanse that descends to the canyon floor below. You might imagine that she gets her diminutive size from the thinner air at this height, like a person starved for oxygen on top of a mountain, or from buffeting by the elements. After all, most wild cacao trees naturally grows in sheltered forest lowlands, often near riverbanks, not even close to this height. But here in this isolated corner of northern Peru, ancient cacao seem happy to grow well up the 6,000-mile-high canyon wall. Some of the most remarkable specimens of all cluster thickly on a patch of ground 4,100 feet up, something that was long thought by cacao experts to be impossible. Here in this canyon, some old assumptions seem not to apply.

Here is the farm of Don Fortunato, home to the single tree that genetic analysis has shown to be the purest example of a very old strain of cacao that was

Don Fortunato transports sacks of cacao beans using burro power. Some of the beans are shown in a cross-section in the foreground.

thought, until recently, to have gone extinct. Cuttings from this mother tree have been used to create thousands more like her, now growing to maturity in this isolated canyon.

Don Fortunato — "Don" is not his first name, but a title of respect in Spanish — is custodian of the now celebrated mother tree that bears his name — Fortunato No. 4. The weathered farmer, a thin, fit man in his fifties, has earned the respect of his neighbors and so most often goes by the honorary title. He's been farming this ground for more than thirty years — not far from the place where, nearly five hundred years ago, the doomed king of the Incas was ambushed and his warriors slaughtered by the conquistador Pizarro and his men.

In his time here, Don Fortunato has seen many changes take place on this land, from the commonplace cultivation of indigenous cacao, and of the coffee bean and fruit crops he still grows, to more recent times, when rice was planted everywhere. Farmers were subsidized by the government to grow it in order to feed a poor, hungry population. At the same time, fields of native cacao were often pushed aside in favor of more modern cacao hybrids that were developed to increase harvests without much regard to the flavor of the chocolate that was produced from their seeds. The new hybrid cacao, called CCN-51, a high-yielding, fast-growing variety that most people agree results in inferior-tasting chocolate, was introduced in Peru in 2002 by the U.S. Agency for International Development as part of the U.S. war on drugs. The purpose was to give farmers a profitable alternative to growing coca, the active ingredient in cocaine.

///////////////

Coca has never been a main crop in this corner of the Marañón River valley, but in other parts of the country, it was key. Indigenous people of Peru, since long before the days of the Inca Empire, have traditionally chewed the leaves of the coca plant, which contain the alkaloid erythroxylum, which differs from cacao's primary alkaloid, theobromine. Both alkaloids are stimulants when consumed by humans and other animals, with similar mild effects, unlike cocaine— the much more powerful, highly refined, and illegal, drug that can be made from coca leaves. Coca leaf consumption has long been an integral part of Andean cultural traditions. The plant is widely used as an energizer, and for medicinal, sacred, and social purposes, much as cacao was traditionally used in Mesoamerica.

Peru and its neighbor country Colombia are the world's largest producers of cocaine, and the U.S. government knows that farmers who can be persuaded to abandon planting coca are likely to choose the highest-yielding alternative crops. What many farmers don't realize is that CCN-51 cacao, like rice, can only be successfully grown with the extensive use of fertilizers that most poor farmers can't afford to buy. When Peruvian farmers took to growing CCN-51, it rapidly depleted their soil and withered away, leaving them with little or nothing. Native cacao, on the other hand, perfectly adapted to the soil in which it has grown for centuries, needs no fertilizer to thrive. Even at 3,500 feet and higher.

Don Fortunato grows his cacao the old-fashioned way. He never fertilizes his trees and rarely even trims them. Some members of the local cacao growers' association joke that Don Fortunato would no sooner cut the branches of his trees than he would lop off the limbs of his children. And yet his cacao trees, as renowned as they've recently become in the world of fine chocolate, aren't even his main crop; coffee is. He also cultivates a long list of other plants: limes, lemons, grapefruit, oranges, mangoes, sugar cane, alfalfa, coconuts, chili peppers, sapote, guaba, and three varieties of banana trees, which help to shelter his young cacao trees from the punishing sun. He keeps bees for their honey, a burro or two for carrying things up and down steep mountain paths, an assortment of other livestock, fowl, and a number of dogs and cats who roam at will.

Leaves, dead branches, and fallen pods litter the ground beneath his cacao trees, along with any other organic material that happens to land there; these materials fertilize the trees and encourage midges to visit his cacao flowers. It's the natural way for cacao, and Don Fortunato's trees are like those that have always grown here, not the creation of a lab. Growing in this remote location, tucked away in a steep mountain canyon with its own protected microclimate, separated from the hybrids and mongrel trees introduced through the years, these cacao trees might be the descendants of those the Spanish found growing near here when they first set foot on this land centuries ago. Fortunato himself is descended, at least in part, from the natives who originally grew those trees. Like most Peruvians, his ancestry is a mix of Indian and Spanish.

Not far away, Peruvian Indians still live deep in the rainforest, in hidden places where they retreated when the government opened the canyon to subsidized homesteading back in the 1960s. It was then that Don Fortunato came here as a child, along with his family. Less than twenty miles from here these indigenous people, the Aguaruna (sometimes called Awajun) still hunt with blowguns, living simply as hunter-gatherers and farmers. Fiercely independent, they were never subjugated by either the Incas or the Spanish; many speak neither English nor Spanish, only their native tongue, and in most cases, they've never seen a another human being outside of their tribe—let alone a white man.

The shadows of the past run long and deep here.

//////////////

Dan Pearson and Brian Horsley are Americans who knew nothing of cacao when they first came to this canyon in 2002. Dan was an investment banker from California, Brian his stepson from a former marriage. They were working for the largest gold mine in Cajamarca, the historic city built over the ancient site where the Inca king Atawallpa was detained by Pizarro and, bargaining for his life and his kingdom, agreed to turn over all the gold in Qosqo to the Spanish invaders. More than five hundred years later, gold is still being dug out of the Cajamarca mountains.

Dan had tried once to retire, but he found himself

bored and restless, and then a chance visit to a friend had brought him to this area. By 2009, he and Brian were working as contractors for the mine, providing everything from needed machine parts to fresh fruits and vegetables for the miners.

Dan wasn't thinking about chocolate on the day he first spotted a cacao tree; he was thinking about bananas. But what he found while visiting a banana grove, looking for fresh fruit for the miners, changed his life and Brian's profoundly, and today he says, "I don't believe in coincidence." What happened that day in the Marañón Canyon, he thinks, was som›ow meant to happen.

The mine owners had requested fresh tropical fruit, hard to come by in such a remote location. Dan and Brian had gone to inquire at the agricultural office in a nearby town, where they happened to meet a friendly local farmer par excellence by the name of Noe (pro-nounced No-ay), who just happened to be doing business at the ag office that day.

Bananas? No problem! He took the two Americans on a short tour, although it turned out to be twice as long in the hot, humid jungle as he'd led them to believe. They had to cross the swelling, swirling Marañón River, but once they were in the canyon, Noe's farm was but a short distance away.

The Marañón River winds through a lush Andean valley in Peru on its way to help form the headwaters of the mighty Amazon.

There were the bananas, one of Noe's many crops. Dan, taking it all in, noticed a smallish tree huddled under taller, tree-size banana plants. The smaller tree displayed a strange, bright yellow fruit shaped like a grooved football and sprouting straight from the tree's main trunk.

"What's that?" Dan asked Noe.

"Cacao" was the reply. Otherwise known as cocoa, otherwise known as . . . chocolate!

Dan had never imagined that the chocolate bars

he'd seen and eaten his whole life could come from something that looked like *this*. How could that be? Noe obliged by cutting down a pod and opening it so Dan could see what was inside: a thick, whitish, juicy pulp embedded with large, almond-shaped seeds arranged in orderly rows. Dan touched the pulp, and smelled it. Noe assured him it was good to eat, so he tried a taste, and was instantly hooked. The stuff was good! Sweet and refreshing, a little like lemonade, but with a bit more tang. The seeds were too bitter to eat, said Noe, but Dan was interested in them, especially because they weren't all the same color. Some of the seeds were purple, and less than half were white. Dan wondered what that meant.

//////////////

The fact that he and Brian had found themselves here at all that day was improbable. It was such a remote location, hard to get to even in good weather, all but impossible in bad. The rainy season stretches, on average, from November to April. The canyon is a triangle that rises twelve miles from each bank of the river, just one of many deeply eroded valleys along the thousand-mile stretch of the Marañón—which winds around the foothills of the Andes before turning east and cutting through mountains to join the Ucayali River, ultimately merging with it to form the headwaters of the Amazon. The journey to this place involves a mind-numbing, bone-jarring series of airplanes, bumpy but breathtaking drives through the Andes, a river crossing via flat barge or long boat (depending on recent rains and the river), and then more driving (if you're lucky, in 4x4 v>icles) high up into the forest and countryside. Arriving here by chance is, to say the least, unlikely.

Dan couldn't get the cacao fruit, and its seeds, out of his mind, so in the following days and weeks, he set about learning everything he could about them. He collected some basic information: The delicious pulp, while it is used in Peru for various drinks, including a fermented sort of wine, is of only secondary importance to the bitter seeds. But for the seeds to be edible, they must first be separated from the pulp, or better yet, be allowed to ferment naturally with the pulp attached for a few days before being dried. Then the thin husk that surrounds each seed must be removed — pared away, the way one might skin an onion — before they're fit to eat. They're not yet chocolate, but they're worthy of attention.

Dan managed to take a few beans with him when he returned to California.

Back home, he found he *liked* these beans, all by themselves. They seemed to give him extra energy when he popped a few into his mouth before heading to the gym to work out. He researched the chemical properties of cocoa beans and learned that they contain hundreds of distinct chemical compounds. He investigated the health claims made for them, and he also learned that a growing market was emerging in the Western world for premium, Fair Trade, and organic chocolate.

Ever on the lookout for a good business opportunity, he dug deeper. Again he wondered why these beans came in a mix of purple and white, at the ratio of about 60 to 40 percent.

There must be experts who could give him some answers, he thought, and now that he was back in the modern world, with reliable electricity and an Internet connection, they would be just a mouse click away. He'd already been networking like crazy, attending chocolate shows, conferences, tastings, and conventions — anywhere he could go to get up to speed on what was turning out to be a much more complicated subject than he'd ever imagined when tearing open a Hershey bar back in the day.

As part of his research, Dan traveled to New York City to attend the annual meeting of the Fine Chocolate Industry Association (FCIA), where he found himself wading into a subculture that felt as strange, in its way, as stepping back in time into the Marañón canyon community had. He met Gary Guittard, a fourth-generation chocolate maker whose great-grandfather had come from France to San Francisco for the gold rush and instead had wound up, in 1868, founding the family business. The two men began talking, one thing led to another, and Dan ended up handing over a small bag of Marañón Canyon cocoa beans.

Could Guittard, possibly, create a test batch of chocolate from these beans? He could.

The results, two wefis later, were interesting but . . . disappointing. *Very* disappointing. After the prototype had been subjected to an official "tasting," Dan was advised that the excessively astringent and acidic taste of his chocolate most likely had to do with the fermentation of the beans, not the beans themselves. That only prodded him to delve into the mysteries of fermentation.

///////////////

All this time, as 2009 turned into 2010, Brian had been busy with his own research back in the canyon. By this time, he'd met and fallen in love with a Peruvian woman named Cecelia who worked in finance for the mine; they soon married and settled down in the area.

Life in this place, Brian found, was so different from life back in the States. Here, meals were cooked on wood-fueled stoves and electricity was still a novelty, not yet widely available. Life was simple in many ways but hard in others. Living among the farmers, Brian began to understand how cacao was grown and processed, and he also began to absorb the community itself. The people. He had met many generous people who had helped him learn, and he had forged both a working relationship and a deep friendship with Noe, the smart, hard-working farmer with a young family and deep roots right here. The friend who had started it all. Noe had introduced him to other local cacao growers, including Don Fortunato, known for his long experience and for the quality of the beans he grew.

Brian and Noe had big plans for Marañón canyon cacao: For starters, they'd drawn up blueprints for a central processing facility, close to where the cacao was harvested. A laboratory of sorts: a place to perfect a way to ferment purple and white beans together, even though the optimal fermentation time for the two types normally differs by several days. It took more

Noe stands with one of the young cacao saplings he tends.

expert advice, two years, and eighty-one trial runs, but eventually they got it right.

Finally another testing panel would agree: this was some special chocolate.

At the FCIA conference in New York, Dan had learned, among other things, that the buzz in fine chocolate was beginning to shift from "single origin" to a new focus on genetics. His Google searches had already taught him that white cacao beans are rare. And Brian and Noe had compiled a list of ten markers for identifying different varieties and flavor profiles just from the external appearance of the pods. DNA testing was the next, crucial step forward. To Dan, the possibilities were as exciting as they were overwhelming. He wasn't a scientist, but he needed one. He had to know more.

His quest now led him to the USDA/ARS, and on his computer screen he noted two locations: Beltsville, Maryland, and Miami, Florida. Beltsville came first; he clicked and then he dialed. As it happened, Dr. Lyndel Meinhardt was in his office and his secretary was not. Lyndel picked up the phone. From Dan's point of view, it was perfect: Lyndel Meinhardt, head of the USDA's Sustainable Perennial Crops Lab, and a leading expert on all things chocolate from a scientific perspective.

Dan explained that he'd come upon some cacao trees in northern Peru that contained a 60/40 mix of purple and white beans. Lyndel was interested; he offered that in association with the USDA's research station at Tarapoto in northern Peru, he and his colleagues had been actively exploring the smaller river systems in that area in search of new, original varieties of wild cacao.

Dan mentioned that while Tarapoto was not far from the cacao in question as the crow flies, getting to the research station there might take some doing from the farm where these trees were growing—Fortunato's farm, at 3,500 feet, and no way to get down except by rough, barely navigable roads.

Lyndel thought he'd heard wrong.

"Cacao doesn't grow much over two thousand feet," he pointed out.

"This cacao does," said Dan.

///////////////

Lyndel knew that cacao that grew at such high altitudes was rumored to exist in that part of Peru; it had been described as far back as the time of F. J. Pound's 1938 expedition, when Pound described seeing wild cacao trees at this elevation. But there'd been no further proof, and no one at the USDA had ever seen them.

By now, Dan was primed with the promise of genetic testing for these curious trees. He wanted to know what he had—or rather, what Fortunato had—and perhaps because he was so new to the chocolate business, he wasn't afraid of the answers that might come. Unlike big companies like Hershey and Mars, what did he have to lose?

Lyndel readily agreed to the testing and gave Dan instructions for how to collect and prepare leaf samples to send to Tarapoto for preliminary evaluation. Back in the canyon, samples were gathered and sent. Soon Lyndel asked for more samples, and this time, he wanted them sent to the Beltsville headquarters for confirmation.

Confirmation? Hmm, thought Dan. It was clearly time to head back to Peru.

///////////////

Dan, Brian, and their new friends in the tiny agricultural community of the Marañón canyon region shifted into high gear. They gathered leaves from random cacao trees, labeled them, and plotted their locations with a GPS device. They dried the leaves and dropped them into sealed pouches with silicon packets to keep them fresh. They filled out all the required paperwork for exporting agricultural material. At Fortunato's farm, their new right-hand man, Noe— experienced agriculturalist, jack-of-all-trades, and indispensable community resource—took a liking to that one, scrawny tree off to the side. From outward appearances, she promised nothing. He picked some leaves from her branches, untroubled by the laughter of the others. There was something about the tree, he thought; never mind her unimpressive exterior. It might have been her thin-walled pods, the better to conserve energy for the seeds themselves, the more room left for bigger beans inside. Something.

If anyone knew cacao trees, it was Noe, who still tended his own thriving crop nearby, besides helping with Dan and Brian's new venture. So the scrawny tree's leaves went into a pouch, duly labeled.

White
Beans

*A cacao pod is filled with sweet, whitish,
viscous pulp embedded with seeds. Inside
these seeds are the beans. You cannot
easily tell which pods or seeds will have
white beans, but Mr. Pearson said, without
revealing more, that he has figured it out.*

—Florence Fabricant, *New York Times*, January 11, 2011

"Are you sitting down, Dan?"

It was August 7, 2009, and the call was from Lyndel
Meinhardt in Beltsville. Dan was sitting down.

"What you have here," said Lyndel, "is thought to
be extinct."

Two months of DNA testing by Dr. Dapeng Zhang,
lead geneticist at Beltsville, had startled the scientists. Dan could hear the underlying excitement in the
voice at the other end of the line.

"It's pure Nacional," Lyndel continued. "An identical match to the original variety."

Dan took a moment to let the news sink in. He thought

about other extinct things in the world: dinosaurs, saber-toothed tigers. The dodo and the passenger pigeon. Living species that once walked the earth and flew the skies, and are now only a memory. This cacao that he and Brian had stumbled upon was like that, in a way. This was big.

//////////////

As cacao orchards declined in Mesoamerica in the seventeenth and eighteenth centuries, Nacional's fortunes rose. It was "discovered" in natural groves in Ecuador then, but it could actually be traced back to the early 1600s, if not earlier. With a distinct, naturally sweet, fruity and floral flavor, it became a major alternative to the scarce Criollo of Venezuela and the inferior-quality varieties of Forastero from Ecuador's Gulf Coast. Pure Nacional dominated fine chocolate markets in Europe and the Americas for more than a hundred years. But by 1916, the entire crop had been devastated by disease, and foreign varieties introduced in a largely futile effort to counter the dreaded witches' broom infestation had not lived up to expectations. Like so many other extinct species on earth, pure Nacional was thought to be gone forever.

Until now.

When compared with samples of the pure Nacional genotype compiled from the twelve major germplasm repositories throughout the Americas — containing 5,500 DNA-verified cacao genotypes — the cacao samples Dan had sent from the Marañón River canyon region were clearly identical. The most perfect match of all was the fourth of five trees sampled from Fortunato's farm — the scrawny tree that Noe had singled out. Fortunato No. 4. The mother tree, purest of the pure.

At the Sustainable Perennial Crops Laboratory in Beltsville, Maryland, technician Stephen Pinney (right) and visiting scientist Kun Ji prepare cacao leaf samples for DNA profiling.

A sobering truth lies behind these scientific explorations and this genetic testing; worldwide, cacao is in trouble. It's not just under siege from devastating diseases. Political instability in the countries where it grows, poor infrastructure, corruption, environmental degradation, and climate change all add to the trouble. Certain treasured varieties, especially, are vanishing at an alarming rate. On the flip side, unknown but potentially irreplaceable subgroups that have not yet been documented in their places of origin could disappear before they're even discovered. The chocolate industry, otherwise known as Big Candy, has been worried for some time about its supply chain— worried enough to put its money behind some of the new research. The concern is shared by scientists and chocolate insiders. It's only a matter of time before a world without chocolate could become a reality.

The loss of its fabled pure Nacional cacao was a huge blow to Ecuador economically. This cacao had long been a great source of national pride as well. But genetic testing of modern samples taken from eleven thousand Ecuadorian trees revealed that only six fit the profile of true Nacional, and none of these was even under cultivation. Smothered by introduced hybrids and clones, Ecuador's pure Nacional was all but gone. In contrast, every single leaf sample taken from cacao groves in different locations and altitudes around Peru's Marañón River, both purple seeds and white, had tested positive for genuine Nacional. And the most surprising of all, to Lyndel, had been the trees bearing pods filled with all-white beans, growing at an unheard of altitude of up to 4,600 feet.

Brian had discovered these trees on another farm in the canyon — the farm of Emberto Hernández and his large family — after hearing rumors of their existence. The farmer had been within a week of cutting the trees down, explaining that he didn't care for the naturally sweet flavor of the beans, which lacked cacao's signature bitter undertones. Brian had persuaded him to spare the twenty-three gnarled trees; through cloning, they've since given birth to a thriving grove of twelve thousand that will bear pure white Nacional beans.

Trees like these apparently grow nowhere else on the planet. But there was more. In another pocket of the canyon, Noe had shown Brian some trees that would prove, on testing, to be just as interesting. Their seeds were, it turned out, the perfect cross: half pure Nacional, half the once prized and always rare Criollo.

Why are white beans so special? Lyndel explained to Dan that white beans have fewer bitter compounds called anthocyanins than do the darker purple beans, and therefore they produce a more mellow-tasting, less acidic chocolate. They're the result of mutations that occur when trees are left undisturbed and isolated for hundreds of years. Pods filled with all-white beans are extremely rare; growing at more than four thousand feet — even approaching five thousand feet — they're unprecedented. Before these beans from this part of Peru were discovered, no one knew they existed anywhere in the world.

Why did cacao trees evolve purple seeds instead of white? Scientists think the bitter purple seeds gave an advantage to trees, because predators such as monkeys would spit them out, in that way propagating the cacao.

This would mean that all-white seeds came first, and that *all* cacao trees of every type may have originally produced white seeds.

PRESERVING ANCIENT CACAO TREES

It's easy to forget that chocolate is an agricultural product, just as it's easy to forget that neatly packaged meat in the supermarket's refrigerated compartment was once part of an animal that was raised by farmers. It's easy to forget that cheap chocolate represents just as many hours of labor and as much expense as more expensive chocolate on the small, steamy farms where it originates. It's easier, sometimes, for farmers who are struggling to grow delicate, fine-flavor cacao trees to switch to high-yield hybrids, or to switch crops altogether. Or worse, to sell their land rights to oil companies or mining operations.

Enter the Heirloom Cacao Preservation Initiative, a partnership between the Fine Chocolate Industry Association and the USDA's Agricultural Research Service, launched in 2012 with the goal of creating the first genotype map to focus on fine-flavor cacao trees. Cocoa beans submitted anonymously by growers will be flavor tested by a panel of experienced industry professionals, and those that are considered heirloom quality will have their genomes mapped for future breeding. All information about endangered varieties, even in remote places, will be welcomed, so that these rare cacao trees can be sought out and tested. The partnership aims to identify varieties from around the world that provide the most flavorful chocolate; to link their flavor profiles with genetics in order to propagate these trees naturally for today's chocolate lovers and future generations; and to recognize and reward the farmers who grow these varieties.

/////////////////

Lyndel Meinhardt (left) and Dapeng Zhang examine young cacao trees that are growing in a greenhouse at the USDA/ARS facility in Beltsville, Maryland.

The pure white seeds in cacao pods that grow in Peru are hugely significant for chocolate scientists. The seeds signify that these cacao trees are indigenous to Peru—in other words, that they most likely grew first in Peru. This is a difficult reality for Ecuador's cacao industry to confront. Ecuador's own cacao crops have been languishing. So many hybrids have been introduced that it's hard to find much of the old Nacional anymore. Before it was discovered in 2009 that pure Nacional cacao was growing in Peru,

Ecuador had no incentive to change, and by then environmental degradation resulting from oil drilling and other activities had severely damaged what cacao groves remained there.

The discovery of indigenous Nacional cacao by a rival economy may prove to be key in jump-starting Ecuador's faltering cacao crop. If so, it will give new hope to the country's struggling farmers and, just maybe, lead to long-needed environmental and economic reforms.

Never underestimate the power of chocolate to change the world.

///////////////

High in the Marañón River canyon of Peru, ancient cacao trees grow as they have for so long. On Don Fortunato's farm, the pods are ripening from green to a rainbow of yellow, orange, and purplish brown. Inside the pods' sweet pulp, orderly rows of purple and white beans are growing, storing up nutrients. As the rains begin each November, tiny new flowers will cluster on trunks and main branches, and by December the harvest will begin—almost round-the-clock work in the cacao groves every two wefis until the dry season returns in April.

Don Fortunato and Dan Pearson check on Fortunato's thriving cacao trees, growing high up on the walls of a remote Marañón River canyon.

Dan Pearson and Brian Horsley will be working alongside the farm families in their fields, and with other local men and women in the processing plant nearby. Because their company's chocolate has been featured in a flurry of media coverage and received critical acclaim, chocolate makers from all over the world who buy Marañón chocolate beans will come to visit, braving the sometimes powerful waters of the river crossing that carries them into the canyon. They will meet the farmers and their families, and walk beneath the dappled shade of tall fruit trees, ducking under coffee and cacao branches, listening to dried leaves rustling and crackling under each step, and to the low hum of cicadas overhead.

In the canyon, life is good, and it's getting better. Roads are still impossible during the rainy months,

A young member of the Marañón canyon community samples chocolate made from locally grown cacao beans. In many regions, workers and their families have never tasted chocolate.

but the use of electricity is slowly increasing. Discover-Hope, a nonprofit foundation that Marañón Chocolate helped develop, provides microcredit, education, and training to impoverished women, with the aim of having positive long-term effects on their families and communities.

Crossing the Marañón River into the canyon is still like stepping back in time. Most women there rely on wood fires for cooking, creating a high demand for scarce firewood and causing respiratory and skin problems by polluting the air with smoke. A new partnership between Marañón Chocolate and the Marañón Canyon Cacao Growers Association aims to solve that problem and another, equally vexing one by providing rice husk–burning stoves to needy families in the canyon. Rice is ubiquitous in the region, but the milling process for this grain leaves large mounds of discarded husks that can accumulate for years. Sometimes the husk piles spontaneously ignite into long-smoldering fires that produce high levels of toxic smoke and silica ash, and create even worse respiratory problems than the wood stoves in most family homes. With these simple rice-burning stoves, a serious local hazard will be transformed into a valuable, free resource for families.

In the canyon, it's looking like a very good year for chocolate.

EVERYTHING OLD IS NEW AGAIN

In southern Ecuador, along the eastern slopes of the Andes near the Peruvian border, are the tangible remains of a 5,500-year-old ceremonial center, discovered only a decade ago in a place where archaeologists had not expected such a find. This ruin was once what has been named the Mayo Chinchipe culture: it is located at the base of the "cloud forest"—the transition zone between the highlands and the Amazon lowlands. It spreads over a large area from the tropical rainforest at the headwaters of the Chinchipe River, descending more than 3,500 feet to the point where it empties into the Marañón River near the modern center of Bagua, Peru. Within the circular stone walls of a once sophisticated architectural complex, scientists found ceramic and stone containers and, using modern carbon dating, identified traces of an ancient South American diet: peppers, beans, cassava, yams, sweet potatoes, corn, coca, and cacao.

The telltale markers—theobromine and caffeine—left little doubt that these vessels held some form of cacao. Speculation is that it was Nacional. If verified, this could mean that members of one of the first great Andean civilizations in the Upper Amazon Basin could

have been drinking chocolate made from Nacional cocoa beans long before they were called Nacional, although the cacao could also have been consumed in
some other form. It's clear that Andeans harvested
and processed cocoa beans in the very region where
scientists now agree that *T. cacao* first grew, more than
a thousand years before the Olmec began cultivating
it in the lowlands of Mexico. Cacao trees must have
been thriving, even then, at an elevation of 3,500 feet
above sea level, far higher than their previously known
habitat.

Ancient artifacts and modern science sometimes
intersect, collapsing millennia of human and botanical
history. With this discovery, the long story of chocolate is revised once again, written without words on a
freeform, long-necked ceramic pitcher molded in the
shape of a human face that stares, unblinking, into the
future. Other ancient village sites — including at least
one in northern Peru, on the other side of a national
border that didn't exist for the Mayo Chinchipe — are
also being excavated and painstakingly sifted through
for clues.

If the Mayo Chinchipe people had a processed cacao
beverage 5,500 years ago in southern Ecuador, how
might it have turned up in Mesoamerica more than a
thousand years later? Were cacao seeds traded that
long ago, passed like treasures among some of the
earliest settled humans in the Americas, exchanged for
prized seashells that have been found throughout the
Chinchipe Basin? Could the cocoa beans have traveled

This ceramic vessel, found in Ecuador near the Peruvian border, is more than five thousand years old. Chemical analysis has shown that it once held *Theobroma* cacao, most likely in liquid form.

this way, from the Amazon to the Pacific coast, and eventually, years later, farther north to Mesoamerica? Perhaps when the Mesoamericans first came to value cacao, it had already been traded for centuries by peo ple who had lived in the Amazon rainforest for longer than anyone could remember.

And if *this* is so, it should have come as no surprise that cacao residue also turned up in twelve-hundred-year-old pottery bowls that were excavated in the 1930s from an ancient village site in present-day Utah, near Canyonlands National Park. But it *did* come as a surprise. Some archaeologists were intrigued; others were skeptical. This is the earliest known evidence of possible chocolate in North America, and if confirmed, it challenges a long-held view among archaeologists that early people of the American Southwest had little interaction with their Mesoamerican neighbors. Before this find, the only evidence of trade between the Americas had been the remains of a small quantity of parrots, some copper bells, and seashells. But if processed cacao found its way north of the border, what else came with it? Maybe trade networks were far more extensive than anyone knew. Maybe the Mesoamericans taught their northern neighbors how to use the cacao bean, and much more.

Would cacao have been consumed as a simple food then, ground up into cakes, or would the ritual uses of the Mesoamericans, complete with mandatory foam on top, have traveled with the beans? The mysteries of chocolate, ancient trade routes, and human civilizations begin slowly emerging from water swirled in bowls of weathered pottery, and analyzed by means of high-resolution liquid chromatography–mass spectrometry.

RECIPE

Vegetarian Chili with Chocolate

1 tablespoon olive oil

1 clove garlic, minced

1 small onion, finely chopped

1 green bell pepper, cut into ¼-inch dice

2 tomatoes, cut into ½-inch dice, or one
16-ounce can diced tomatoes

2 15-ounce cans chickpeas, drained and
rinsed

1 15-ounce can *kidney beans*, drained and
rinsed

5 cups *vegetable broth*

2 teaspoons ground cumin

1 teaspoon salt

1½ ounces bittersweet chocolate

❖ *In a stockpot, over medium heat, cook the oil,
garlic, onion, and green pepper until slightly softened, stirring occasionally, about 5 minutes. Add
the tomatoes, chickpeas, kidney beans, vegetable
broth, cumin, and salt. Bring to a boil over high
heat. Reduce heat to low, cover, and simmer, stirring occasionally, until thickened, 1 to 1½ hours.
Before serving, stir in chocolate until melted.*

Chocolate
Rainforests

The rainforest then equals a preserve, the planet's greatest archive of life on Earth with forest-dwellers being humanity's ambassadors to the great outdoors whom we lose only at our own impoverishment.

—Mark Christian, founder of the C-Spot chocolate blog

In the Amazon rainforest, life is bursting out everywhere. The air is alive with bird song and chirping insects, and in every direction you look, shiny leaves in all shades of green filter dappled sunlight across the forest floor. In some places, cacao trees bask in the shade of taller fruit trees and towering hardwoods. Their pods, heavy with seeds and pulp, jut out from the trunks of the trees like bright jewels.

Fifty percent of the world's animal and plant species live in the rainforest, but the rainforest is shrinking. Once it covered 14 percent of the earth's land surface, but now it makes up a mere 6 percent, and the rate at which it is vanishing leads some experts to predict that the last remaining rainforests could

Water tumbles down a mountainside in the Peruvian rainforest.

disappear in less than forty years. They're being destroyed because the value of rainforest land is seen as only the value of its timber and crop fields by shortsighted governments, multinational companies, and desperate landowners. Once the forest is cleared for timber, often by slash-and-burn methods, farming and ranching operations move in, and the rich biodiversity of this ecosystem is further lost. Every time a tree is burned, the carbon stored within it is released into the atmosphere, and a warming planet gets just a little bit warmer.

Five centuries ago, some 10 million Indians lived in the Amazon rainforest, but today, fewer than two hundred thousand Indians reside there. As rainforest peoples are lost, so are centuries of accumulated knowledge of the medicinal value of rainforest species. This is important: the U.S. National Cancer Institute, for example, has identified three thousand plants that actively work against cancer cells, and 70 percent of them are found in the rainforest. Many ingredients of lifesaving prescription drugs are found *only* in the rainforest; thousands of other plants with potential as medicines have yet to be studied.

But the destruction of rainforests endangers the health of Earth in even more fundamental ways. The Amazon rainforest has been called the "lungs of the

Severe deforestation of the Amazon rainforest results in bleak scenes like this one.

planet" because it continuously recycles carbon dioxide into oxygen. More than 20 percent of the world's oxygen is produced in the rainforest, and the Amazon Basin contains one-fifth of the world's fresh water.

///////////////////

For more than fifteen hundred years in Brazil, rainforest farmers practiced a sophisticated kind of forest agriculture. They dug large-scale irrigation systems, integrated and rotated crops, and carried out controlled burning of vegetative cover in order to enrich the soil. They composted, recycled, and built artificial ponds in their wetlands for farming fish. Deep in the forest, they hunted and foraged for medicinal plants and tropical fruits. They harvested wild grasses to cover their sturdy thatched houses, which they built in circular fashion around large, central plazas. They built wide, straight roads that crisscrossed the jungle and connected them with neighboring villages, fishing areas, and hunting grounds.

The European settlers who came beginning in the sixteenth century knew nothing of all this. They quickly began to plunder the forest for its wood, and cleared fields to create pastureland and orderly rows of crops. It's an approach that has continued ever since. Now farmers are the only people who might be able to reverse it, but they need a reason to change course.

Once not so long ago, cacao was grown in abundance in the rainforest, but devastating plant diseases and sinking prices in the world cacao market turned farmers to other, quicker ways to make a living from their land. Could chocolate be the key to preserving this precious, threatened ecosystem, and to helping the people whose livelihood depends on it?

The fact is, chocolate is in trouble too, and it needs the rainforest to survive. That's where its diversity is stored—diversity that is disappearing with every forest acre that is destroyed.

How could chocolate help save the endangered rainforest? In the first place, cacao is a "high-value" crop, or, to put it another way, it's hard to find anyone who doesn't claim to love it. So the demand for chocolate is undiminished. Second, it grows best under a rainforest canopy. It loves shade, so farmers don't have to clear their forestland to grow it; it prefers nesting under other trees. The cacao tree likes things a little messy; it needs the tiny midges that are attracted to natural organic litter on the forest floor to pollinate its flowers, and it stays healthier in the disorderly profusion of mixed rainforest trees than in neat, precise rows of its own kind. It thrives in a kind of orderly disorder, in which a cooperative relationship with nature is most profitable.

In eastern Brazil, some cacao growers are now using a method called *cabruca* that is not so different

SAVE THE EARTH
It's the Only Planet With Chocolate

from the sustainable agroforestry practiced centuries ago by indigenous rainforest dwellers. It involves thinning out just a few of the tall rainforest trees on their land and planting the smaller cacao trees beneath them. Though farmers get fewer cacao trees per acre with this method than with today's more conventional monoculture plantations, the trees are less susceptible to disease and destructive insects and therefore yield more cocoa beans. Pollination rates are higher too. Pesticides and fertilizers are unnecessary, so the beans are 100 percent organic, which provides farmers with an economic advantage. Organic, artisanal, and environmentally friendly chocolate is one of the fastest-growing sectors of the global food market, and farmers get premium prices for organic beans grown in these "chocolate rainforests." And the rubber trees, cassava, banana, papaya, and other fruit trees that provide shade for tender cacao trees also provide income for the farmer as cash crops — plants that are grown strictly to sell and return a profit, not to feed the producer's animals or family.

Some growers are going a step further. They buy depleted and abandoned cocoa plantations and convert them to healthy, productive cabrucas. The conversion process allows farmers to employ many more local people, restore value to land that had been left for dead, and still produce a lot of chocolate. The concept of cabrucas, or chocolate rainforests, is taking root just about anywhere cocoa is grown — even in West Africa, where the Big Candy industry, as we've seen, is responding to public pressure by pledging to source their beans in the future exclusively from Fair Trade or other similarly certified growers.

Sustainable chocolate requires overcoming the disconnect between farmers, chocolate makers, and consumers all over the world. Farmers who have a personal stake in their cacao trees whose prosperity is linked with the sustainability of their trees, and whose intimate knowledge of the trees allows them to provide the very best growing environment for them — can manage disease and pests organically and profitably, one pod at a time. Scientists can help by identifying naturally hardy, flavorful varieties of cacao trees that have thrived in the rainforest for centuries; they can also assist farmers in identifying which fungi are beneficial to cacao trees and which are deadly. Chocolate makers can help by giving more thought to the farmers who grow their beans, and reforming their own practices, to improve the standard of living for these hard-working growers and their families.

Everyone who loves chocolate — and who doesn't?

—can help by learning all we can about the long path our favorite treat travels from pod to bar, and using the power of the purse to support sustainable practices. All of us can start by remembering, each time we bite into a delicious dark bar of fudgy brownie, that it comes from a small forest tree growing in some steamy place far away.

RECIPE

My Grandma Crowell's Fudge Pie

❖ Beat until soft ½ cup butter.

❖ Add 1 cup sugar gradually; blend until creamy. Beat in 2 egg yolks.

❖ Melt, cool slightly, beat in 2 ounces unsweetened chocolate (100% cacao).

❖ Beat ½ cup flour into butter mixture.

❖ Add 1 teaspoon vanilla.

❖ Whip until stiff: 2 egg whites, ⅛ teaspoon salt.

❖ Fold into batter.

❖ Bake in a greased 8–9-inch pie plate at 325 degrees about ½ hour.

❖ Serve with vanilla ice cream (optional).

How to Eat Chocolate

You already knew how to do that, didn't you? But eating chocolate isn't necessarily as simple as it seems. First, there's the question of taste. Most of us prefer the kind of chocolate we were given as children; to our taste, that *is* chocolate. But as Maricel Presilla points out in her delightful book *The New Taste of Chocolate*, these preferences often depend on where one happens to be living at the time of that early experience.

> Americans in blind tastings instinctively go for blends with especially high West African cacao content. This happens to be a dominant cacao in some of the mass-produced brands most Americans have eaten since childhood. . . . On the other hand, Germans tend to hate the intense extra bitter chocolate adored in France. Americans gravitate to very light and French people to very dark

milk chocolate. The Swiss and the Japanese go hand in hand in their love for buttery, high-fat, slick, and satiny chocolate.

Now, as Presilla observes, there's a whole "new school" movement in chocolate tending toward high cocoa content, strong chocolate flavor, and a taste that's more bitter than sweet, even in milk chocolate. For true chocolate connoisseurs, tasting chocolate is a complex process. They recognize that different cocoa beans can have very distinct flavors, depending on a whole host of variables: the variety of bean, the soil and atmosphere, even specific weather conditions at the time of the growing season. Obviously, this degree of chocolate obsession isn't for everyone; some of us just want a brownie now and then!

Taste is the reason most of us eat chocolate, but more and more people are now considering health, sustainability, and human rights in selecting all kinds of foods we eat— including chocolate. For health, experts agree that dark chocolate is best, but not everyone likes the bitter taste of very high cocoa content in their chocolate. If you'd like to transition to dark chocolate, you can do it gradually starting with bars in the 30 to 50 percent dark chocolate range, and trying lots of brands and flavors. So-called fine flavor chocolate is, by definition, more expensive than mass-market chocolate, but it can be more satisfying, and a little can go a long way.

As to sustainability and human justice, history has shown that industries respond to pressure from consumers. All of the major chocolate companies have pledged to eliminate the worst labor abuses from their supply chains by no later than 2020. But promises have been made and broken before.

Reading the label on a chocolate product will tell you a lot. One thing to look for is the designation "organic." This usually means that the cocoa beans used to make the product were not sprayed with pesticides and that they were grown in ways that enriched the forest rather than depleting it. And since practically no inferior-quality bulk cocoa is grown organically, you can be certain that any organic chocolate will have been made from fine flavor beans.

The Fair Trade logo is an indicator of good practices, too, though Fair Trade designations can mean different things. Go to fairtradeamerica.org to learn more.

Many chocolate products have both Fair Trade and organic certifications. Increasingly, however, some of the most responsible and innovative chocolate makers — and many struggling cacao farmers — bypass these certifications, even though their products would qualify them, because the cost of certifying cuts into farmers' incomes and can make it *harder* for them to raise cacao sustainably and humanely.

Knowing all this as you bite into your organic and Fair Trade chocolate bar, you can know that you're doing a little bit to help the world. Now all you have to do is decide which bar tastes the most decidedly delicious!

Chocolate Timeline

8000 B.C.–2000 B.C.(?)

Cacao tree originates in the Amazon Basin of South America.

1500 B.C.–400 B.C.

Olmec civilization of south-central Mexico cultivates cacao as a domestic crop. Evidence of chocolate residue on ceramic vessels suggests pre-Olmec people used cacao beverages as early as 1900 B.C.

A.D. 250–900

Maya of southern Mexico inherit chocolate culture from their Olmec neighbors, greatly expanding its use and importance. Cocoa beans are used to make the prized chocolate drink, as currency, and as a unit of calculation. Cocoa pods symbolize fertility and life, and are often depicted on pottery and other art forms.

1200–1521

Aztec civilization dominates much of Mesoamerica, inherits chocolate from the Maya, adds seasonings, and further expands its importance, including use in religious ritual and sacrifice. Aztec emperor is the first to tax cocoa beans. Consumption of chocolate is limited mostly to the ruling class and military.

1519–1521

Conquistador Hernán Cortés conquers Mexico and establishes a cocoa plantation there in the name of Spain—the beginning of an extremely lucrative business of growing money on trees. After his cousin, conquistador Francisco Pizarro, defeats the Inca king in 1533 and seizes Indian territory in South America, the Spanish and Portuguese soon establish cacao plantations there as well.

1528

Chocolate arrives in Spain and this time it is noticed. Cortés presents the Spanish king, Charles V, with cocoa beans from the New World and the necessary tools for its preparation.

1544

Dominican friars take a delegation of Maya nobles from Mexico to visit Spain's Prince Philip. They present the prince with gift jars of mixed and beaten cocoa, ready to drink. Soon the Spanish add sugar, as well as other flavorings such as vanilla and various spices, and serve it heated, and chocolate becomes beloved by the Spanish nobility. It remains a closely guarded secret in Spain for almost one hundred years.

1569

Pope Pius V declares that drinking chocolate on Friday does not break the Catholic fast.

1615

Anne of Austria, daughter of Philip III of Spain, introduces the chocolate beverage to her new husband, Louis XIII of France, and to the French court.

1657

The first chocolate house is opened in London by a Frenchman. Chocolate houses become the trendy meeting places where elite London society gathers to talk and savor the new luxury sensation.

1753

Swedish naturalist Carl Linnaeus renames the cacao tree *Theobroma cacao*, "food of the gods," in his definitive encyclopedia of scientific taxonomy, *Species Plantarum*.

1755

Chocolate first appears in the English colonies of America, obtained abroad by Benjamin Franklin for soldiers marching in the French and Indian War.

1765

John Hanau and Dr. James Baker establish America's first chocolate factory in Dorchester, Massachusetts. By 1780, the mill is producing Baker's Chocolate.

1795

Dr. Joseph Fry of Bristol, England, uses a steam engine to grind cocoa beans.

1828

The cocoa press is invented by Dutch chemist Coenraad Van Houten, making possible more affordable and smoother, better-tasting chocolate to drink.

1847

Solid eating chocolate is developed by J. S. Fry & Sons, a British chocolate maker.

1875

Daniel Peter of Vevey, Switzerland, teams up with his neighbor, food scientist Henri Nestlé, to perfect the production of milk chocolate, using condensed milk.

1879

Rodolphe Lindt of Berne, Switzerland, invents the conching machine, which heats and rolls liquid chocolate mass to refine it. After chocolate has been conched, more cocoa butter is added, creating the texture that "melts in your mouth."

1895

Milton S. Hershey sells his first Hershey bar in Pennsylvania, using modern mass-production techniques that make chocolate affordable to everyone.

1906

The first known published recipe for chocolate brownies appears in the *Boston Cooking-School Cook Book*, edited by Fanny Merritt Farmer. The recipe calls for two squares of Baker's Chocolate.

1930

Ruth Wakefield runs out of the baking chocolate she uses to make popular cookies for her Toll House Inn, Whitman, Massachusetts, so she improvises by cutting up a semisweet Nestlé's bar and stirring the chunks into her dough. The resulting cookie is so popular that in 1939, Nestlé begins to manufacture little bits of chocolate especially for making Toll House cookies.

1941–1945

At Milton Hershey's suggestion, the American military decides to include three four-ounce chocolate bars, each providing 600 calories, in a soldier's "D-Ration." Although meant to sustain the men (chocolate had also been given to Aztec warriors to fortify them for battle), the bars become a symbol of peace when malnourished victims of war are approached by American soldiers holding out chocolate to them. Chocolate remains standard issue in the military today. It has also traveled into space, as part of the diet of U.S. astronauts.

1964

Publication of British writer Roald Dahl's 1964 book *Charlie and the Chocolate Factory,* on which two movies have been based. During the sweets-loving Dahl's childhood, the two largest British candy firms, Cadbury and Rowntree, sent so many moles to work in competitors' factories that their spying became legendary. This practice was also rumored to have been implemented over the years in the American chocolate rivalries of major companies such as Hershey and Mars.

1980

Life imitates art: chocolate espionage features in the worldwide press after an apprentice of the Swiss company Suchard-Tobler tries unsuccessfully to sell secret chocolate recipes to Russia, China, Saudi Arabia, and other countries.

1990S TO THE PRESENT

In October 2006, the world's tallest chocolate structure is unveiled at the FAO Schwarz toy store in New York City. It stands over twenty feet tall and consists of more than 2,285 pounds of chocolate, thus proving that chocolate is also structurally sound!

Designer chocolate bars appear on the market as "single-origin" bars made from South American cocoa beans, and exotic ingredients, from saffron and curry to goat cheese and basil, are added to high-end bars. Artisan chocolatiers begin offering versions of "Aztec" chocolate, spiced with "New World" flavors such as chili and cinnamon. High-percentage-cacao chocolate is recognized by scientists as a health food owing to its beneficial antioxidants and other nutrients.

Bibliography

The literature of chocolate is as fascinating as it is vast. It contains many more stories than could be told here. If you're interested in learning more, these books provide a window onto a world of knowledge.

Almond, Steve. *Candyfreak: A Journey Through the Chocolate Underbelly of America.* Chapel Hill, N.C.: Algonquin, 2004.

Brenner, Joël Glenn. *The Emperors of Chocolate: Inside the Secret World of Hershey and Mars.* New York: Random House, 1999.

Cadbury, Deborah. *Chocolate Wars: The 150-Year Rivalry Between the World's Greatest Chocolate Makers.* New York: PublicAffairs, 2010.

Coe, Sophie D., and Michael D. Coe. *The True History of Chocolate.* London: Thames & Hudson, 2013.

D'Antonio, Michael. *Hershey: Milton S. Hershey's Extraordinary Life of Wealth, Empire, and Utopian Dreams.* New York: Simon & Schuster, 2006.

Higgs, Catherine. *Chocolate Islands: Cocoa, Slavery, and Colonial Africa.* Athens: Ohio University Press, 2012.

Jacobsen, Rowan. *Chocolate Unwrapped: The Surprising Health Benefits of America's Favorite Passion.* Montpelier, Vt.: Invisible Cities, 2003.

Mann, Charles C. *1491: New Revelations of the Americas Before Columbus.* New York: Knopf, 2012.

Off, Carol. *Bitter Chocolate: The Dark Side of the World's Most Seductive Sweet.* St. Lucia, Australia: University of Queensland, 2008.

Presilla, Maricel E. *The New Taste of Chocolate: A Cultural and Natural History of Cacao with Recipes.* Berkeley, Calif.: Ten Speed Press, 2001.

Ryan, Orla. *Chocolate Nations: Living and Dying for Cocoa in West Africa.* London: Zed Books, 2012.

Williams, Pam, and Jim Eber. *Raising the Bar: The Future of Fine Chocolate.* Vancouver, B.C.: Wilmor Publishing, 2012.

Wilson, Philip K., and W. Jeffrey Hurst. *Chocolate as Medicine: A Quest over the Centuries.* Cambridge, U.K.: Royal Society of Chemistry, 2012.

Young, Allen M. *The Chocolate Tree: A Natural History of Cacao.* Washington, D.C.: Smithsonian Institution Press, 1994.

Websites

The C-Spot

www.c-spot.com

This is an amazing resource. In-depth history, science, reviews, and up-to-the-minute news about all things chocolate. Frequently updated, including an informative newsletter. A good place to start.

Chocolate: Facts, History, and Factory Tour

www.exploratorium.edu/exploring/exploring_chocolate/index.html

Another site packed with information on the history and cultivation of chocolate and on its health effects — plus a video tour of a real chocolate factory.

The Chocolate Life

www.thechocolatelife.com

An online community "for chocophiles and aspiring chocophiles to explore, learn, and share."

Fair Trade America

fairtradeamerica.org

Learn more about how Fair Trade is helping cacao and coffee farmers worldwide.

Fine Chocolate Industry Association
www.finechocolateindustry.org
Learn more about fine chocolate and about the Heirloom Cacao Preservation Initiative.

Harnessing the Power of Plants, Mars Botanical
www.marsbotanical.com
Website for the scientific division of the Mars Company. Learn about leading industry research on flavonols in cocoa, and the new products being developed to take advantage of them.

The Hershey Story
www.hersheystory.org
Online exhibits and information about educational activities, events, tastings, and tours at the famed Milton S. Hershey complex in Hershey, Pennsylvania.

World Cocoa Foundation
worldcocoafoundation.org
This chocolate industry organization is dedicated to achieving cocoa sustainability and supporting cocoa

communities, education, field programs, and scientific research.

//////////////////

Small chocolate companies are doing some incredible, exciting things today, in so many ways: flavor, innovation, sustainability, and social justice. The companies listed here are just a few noteworthy examples. It's well worth spending some time learning about them (and looking for more). Their websites are interesting and informative, and many have gorgeous photographs. And so many kinds of chocolate to try!

Cacao Prieto

cacaoprieto.com

A Brooklyn, New York–based chocolate maker with family roots in Dominican Republic cacao farming going back to 1899. This inventor and former NASA engineer has teamed with Hershey/Penn State geneticists to harness every part of the cacao tree, making bean-to-bar chocolate, compost from husks and pods, distilled liquors from pulp juices, cocoa butter for cosmetics, and phytonutrients used in pharmaceuticals. Genetics-based cacao breeding, a global lab, and vintage cocoa processing equipment combined with modern versions of the old machines. Lots of interesting stuff here.

Mast Brothers Chocolate

mastbrothers.com

Another unique artisan chocolate maker in Brooklyn, New York. In going back to the future, the brothers have even tried transporting a load of cocoa beans from the Dominican Republic by sailing ship, all the way to a pier in Brooklyn's Red Hook Harbor that had not seen a commercial sailing ship since 1939.

Kallari Cooperative

www.kallari.com

A cooperative of native Ecuadorian cocoa and coffee growers and entrepreneurs who went from selling poorly fermented cocoa beans for low prices to middlemen, to selling properly processed beans directly to major fine chocolate makers, to making their own uniquely fresh chocolate right in Ecuador and marketing it worldwide. The website tells their impressive story.

Liberation Cocoa

www.liberationchocolate.com

A collective of cacao farms in Africa's Liberia committed to economic and social justice, as well as exceptional chocolate. Liberation Cocoa is rehabilitating and reintegrating former child soldiers from this war-torn region and refurbishing abandoned cacao groves into sustainable ecosystems.

Green & Black's Maya Gold (Video)

www.youtube.com/watch?v=-At9adHgXFc

This video shows and tells the story of indigenous Maya from Belize whose ancient Criollo groves were all but destroyed and replaced by "hardy, disease-resistant" clones. When the bottom fell out of the world cocoa market, the Maya were left with almost nothing, until they replanted their ancient native trees and began producing organic Fair Trade bars.

Marañón Chocolate

www.maranonchocolate.com

This extensive website introduces Marañón Chocolate, whose rediscovered pure Nacional cacao from Peru's Marañón River canyon rocked the world of fine chocolate, and is now part of a renaissance in fine chocolate made from what may be akin to the original cocoa beans that first grew in the Upper Amazon Basin of South America thousands of years ago.

Acknowledgments

The idea for this book was born when I came across two news items, one aired on National Public Radio and the other published in the *New York Times*, two institutions that help me, in small ways almost every day, to make sense of the world. The stories concerned the discovery in Peru of a rare, formerly-thought-to-be-extinct type of cacao, the plant from which chocolate is made.

Like many people, I had never given much thought to the vegetable source of chocolate. I had no idea what such a plant might look like and only the vaguest awareness that it grew someplace hot and far away—probably Mexico. The idea of scientists tramping through the Amazon rainforest of Peru searching for wild chocolate (instead of wild animals) captured my imagination. And having recently finished a book about scientists searching for wild ponies in the marshes of Assateague Island, located off the coast of Maryland and Virginia, I could clearly see this one in my mind's eye: *The Chocolate Scientist!* I envisioned a fun, uncomplicated book with lots of eye appeal and, well, taste appeal.

Writing this book did turn out to be great fun — and unexpectedly tasty — but it was anything but uncomplicated.

My wonderful editor at Houghton Mifflin Harcourt, Cynthia Platt, was enthusiastic from the start, but she encouraged me to think about a much bigger, more ambitious book than I'd had in mind — one that would not only encompass fascinating new scientific discoveries but also place them in the context of the centuries-old sweep of chocolate's history — a complex tale of discovery, ambition, greed, piracy, secrecy, exploitation, and innovation that reaches into almost every corner of the world. Writing *that* story was a daunting prospect, to say the least. As neither a trained historian nor a scientist, what could I possibly add, I wondered, to the long list of "big" books about chocolate that were already in the world? I surveyed the field, and found a multitude of scholarly tomes and beautiful coffee-table books aimed at various adult audiences, and another nice selection of slimmer books about chocolate for the youngest readers — but almost nothing in between. So with considerable trepidation, I took the plunge.

Luckily, my research first led me to Lyndel Meinhardt, a leading chocolate scientist but also an unassuming, patient scholar who was generous with his time and with the considerable resources of the USDA/ARS facility in Beltsville, Maryland, which just happens to be not too far from my home in Pennsylvania. I could not have written this book without the thorough foundation that Lyndel provided me with on the subject of chocolate, and I'm especially grateful to him for my first glimpse of real cacao trees growing just north of the Mason-Dixon Line, quite far from their natural equatorial home. If you've never seen one of these trees, they are exotic, colorful, and beautiful to b›old.

The other person mentioned in those NPR and *New York Times* stories was equally gracious and generous when I contacted him. Dan Pearson of Marañón Chocolate so clearly conveyed the excitement he had felt at encountering ancient cacao trees growing in an unexpected place on the edge of the Amazon rainforest of Peru that I felt as if I were right there with him and Brian Horsley in their discovery. I'm deeply grateful, too, for the gorgeous photos Dan made available to me and to this book.

Mark Christian, chocophile extraordinaire and creator of the C-Spot blog, the most incredible resource a chocolate newbie could ask for, was also kind enough to answer all of my questions.

I consulted many books in the vast literature of

chocolate in the course of researching this one. All of them helped me to understand the long and convoluted history, as well as the *natural* history, of this unique food, but I'm especially indebted to three:

The True History of Chocolate, coauthored by Michael D. Coe and his late wife, Sophie D. Coe, provided invaluable context and rich historical detail that brought the subject alive for me. Anyone who thinks history books are dull should read this one! Not only did it inspire me and, at times, dismay and outrage me with a lively narrative that somehow I was never taught in school; it was also my go-to resource for checking dates and names, and for beginning to understand how the early history of chocolate in Mesoamerica indelibly shaped cultures on several continents.

Bitter Chocolate: The Dark Side of the World's Most Seductive Sweet, by Carol Off, provided crucial insights into the long history of human slavery in West Africa's cacao trade (as well as a subliminal title suggestion, apparently). Thank you for a fine example of impassioned, professional journalism, and a Canadian sensibility that made me aware, for the first time, of the wonderfully inspiring children's chocolate strike of 1947.

The Chocolate Tree: A Natural History of Cacao, by

Allen M. Young, whose lyrical yet rigorously scientific book *The Chocolate Tree: A Natural History of Cacao* transported me to a dreamlike chocolate forest, but at the same time told me more than I would have known to ask about the trees and the insects and other wild creatures that make it possible for me, and you, and all of us living far from the steamy groves of cacao trees on the edge of the rainforest to enjoy chocolate nearly any time the fancy strikes.

Finally, a big thanks to my family—Laurel, Will, Erik, and Amanda—who during my work on this book gifted me with more kinds of delicious chocolate than I knew existed, all in the name of "research." And to Lans, who patiently listened to my endless retellings of events and facts that I was discovering for the first time, and who cheerfully sampled all kinds of chocolate, from the strange to the sublime, that somehow found its way into our home over the past many months. It was a tough job, but someone had to do it.

Photo Credits

Ammit/Alamy: 179

ARS: 156, 167, 171, 201, 206

Gerardo Barbolla/Fotolia: 26

Scott Bauer: G, H (insert)

Don Couch/Houghton Mifflin Harcourt: 65, C (insert, top)

De Agostini/Getty Images: 68, D (insert, top)

DEA Picture Library: E (insert)

Alvaro del Campo: 217, N–O, P (insert)

Divine Chocolate, Ltd: 6

Fair Trade USA: 121, B (insert)

Kay Frydenborg: M (insert, bottom)

FValdez IRD France: 213

Getty Images: 93, 130

Peggy Greb: M (insert, top)

Hershey Community Archives: 94, 102

Houghton Mifflin Harcourt: 15, 105, 221

iStockphoto: 11, 31, 49, 67, 110, 128, 145 (top), 150

iStockphoto (Photo by Hulton Archive/Getty Images): 107

Jonathan Kantor/Lifesize/Getty Images: 89

Justin Kerr: D (insert, bottom)

Grigory Kubatyan/Fotolia: 36

Library of Congress: 51

Library of Congress, NY World-Telegram & Sun Collection: 163

Dmitry Mayatsky/Fotolia: 54, F (insert)

Rachel Newborn (graphics): i, 20, 38, 39, 60, 75, 91, 137, 165, A (insert)

Katherine Page/Maranon Chocolate: vi, 14, 23, 181, 188, 194, 208, 209, I, J, K (insert)

Pete Pattisson: 119

Photodisc/Getty Images: 145 (bottom), 219

Pixtal/Age Fotostock: 81

James Rodriguez for Fair Trade USA: 123

Urbanhearts/Fotolia: L (insert, top)

Vancouver Sun: 2

Wikimedia Commons: 17, C (insert, bottom)

Index

Page numbers in **bold** type denote photos and illustrations.